Dear Mr W

Hope that you will
have the best summer
and joy this book from
my grandmother

love will
Hondamwani

PHYLLIS GEORGE

NEVER
say NEVER
YES YOU CAN!

BUTLER BOOKS

ISBN: 978-193549705-9

Printed in Canada

Cover design by Scott Stortz

Published by:

Butler Books
P.O. Box 7311
Louisville, KY 40207
Phone (502) 897-9393
Fax (502) 897-9797

www.butlerbooks.com

To my parents, Bob and Louise, who were always there for me and taught me to believe in myself,

To my children, Lincoln and Pamela, who hopefully will learn from my past and use these lessons in their future,

And to all of those people who told me I could "never" do something. Thank you for challenging me to prove that I could.

CONTENTS

Foreword by Rick Pitino   vi

Introduction   xi

1. Say Yes to Yourself   1

2. Embrace Change as Your Friend   21

3. Be a Risk Taker   35

4. Find a Void and Fill It   51

5. Trust Your Instincts   67

6. Keep Your Options Open   83

7. Feel the Power of Being Nice   97

8. Life Isn't Perfect   111

9. Keep Your Perspective   129

10. Learn to Laugh at Yourself   145

Afterword: In Closing ... a Few More Things   165

Acknowledgments   170

FOREWORD

by Rick Pitino

Phyllis is a pioneer. Her range is what impresses me the most. She entered a highly competitive pageant and emerged as Miss America. She became the first national female sports broadcaster. She flourished in the limelight as First Lady in the state of Kentucky. She's been successful in business. And she is a respected humanitarian.

Each step along the way, she embraced the mission at hand. There is a great deal of doubt and uncertainty when you are a pioneer, no matter how much passion you have, no matter how much knowledge you possess, no matter how much you love what you do. Imagine going through a tunnel, not knowing what is in store for you at the other end—success, failure, or just another path that leads you somewhere else. Phyllis never knew where each of her tunnels would lead.

Phyllis was able to conquer her fears and become successful through a strong work ethic and fervent self-esteem. Her attitude toward each venture she tackled has allowed her to be so diverse. It seems that whatever she takes on, she emerges victorious. Like anyone striving for success, she had to do her research, develop a work plan, and devote herself to a stick-to-it effort.

She opened a door for many women by entering a chauvinistic sports world. At the time she appeared on the scene, there were very few female sports reporters, and there were none on national television. Working with a talented blend of characters who would cut her no slack if she did not know the material, Phyllis had to be knowledgeable, insightful, and powerful. She had to have a strong presence in a very difficult environment.

Phyllis had to be a tremendous risk taker. Had she failed, she would have been ridiculed twice as much as any other broadcaster precisely because she was a pioneer. When you break barriers, you have to be really good at what you do to open doors. You just can't be mediocre. You have to be great. Jackie Robinson opened up so many doors for African-American athletes because he had grit and tremendous talent. It is obvious he made a huge impact. Likewise, Phyllis paved the way for women by being a risk taker.

The lessons Phyllis shares in *Never Say Never* are not only inspirational, helping you understand that you too can succeed, but they're lessons for everybody. It doesn't matter if you're the CEO of a company or a high school or college student just starting out and trying to make it in this world. Her ten lessons are a realistic approach to help anyone succeed in daily life.

Phyllis looks at not taking yourself too seriously. That's a great notion to understand. When you take yourself too seriously, you may start to embrace success, but you lose your creativity and your ability to communicate with people. Then you lose your passion because you start to think you've invented what you've done. If you don't take yourself too seriously, you're on a constant treadmill of learning new things and you never get off the treadmill of learning. You don't want to fall off because you recognize that there's always more to learn. That's what never taking yourself too seriously is all about.

Like many of us in high-profile occupations, Phyllis has experienced her success stories as well as learned how to deal with her failures. Any successful person has had to deal with failure. She learned how to minimize her failures, overcome them, and put them into perspective. You have to understand the big picture of success. Triumphant people do.

One really unique chapter in this book is about the power of being nice. You won't find that in many motivational books. Others talk of power, of making money, and of finding ways to get ahead. Spirituality is mentioned almost universally. But power is an ability to act. If you can impact on the lives of others by making a difference in their lives through being nice, being a leader, or directing them in the right way, you get power from that. You can turn people on by being nice, and that's what we want. So many people turn others off with their attitude. The chapter on feeling the power of being nice is a lesson on how to open up and encourage people to like and respect you.

In *Never Say Never*, the teachings of Norman Vincent Peale, Phyllis's mentor, shine through. His message that you can be successful by taking the criticisms you face, shrinking them down to the size of a pea, and making the positives as grand as the sky, has helped shaped Phyllis's life. You have to have that Norman Vincent Peale attitude to thrive as Phyllis has.

You have to be emotionally tough to succeed. At times you need to have skin as tough as a rhinoceros. Many people may become jealous of you. They often think for some reason that you've achieved something without it being deserved. That's never the case with passionate people. It's always deserved.

And that's a big reason I highly recommend this book, because these lessons are steps to succeeding in a passionate way. It's one thing to be successful, build a degree of wealth, and fulfill the professional dreams you have. But being able to do it with a smile on your face while having a positive impact on people's lives is what separates great leaders from mediocre ones. That's what Phyllis has done.

To be an accomplished person and still have people like and respect you shows that you have staying power. People who have staying power are genuine, and that's what Phyllis George is, genuine!

INTRODUCTION

Hi, I'm Phyllis George. Many of you know me, but perhaps some of you who have heard my name can't quite place when or where.

"Aren't you the one who was married to that senator from Virginia?" is a question I get asked a lot. No, that was Liz Taylor. I was married to the governor of Kentucky.

"Wait, I remember," others say. "You sang so beautifully when you won Miss America." No, that wasn't me. I played the piano.

"I loved watching you on ABC's *Monday Night Football*." Amazing! Especially since I was on CBS's *NFL Today* on Sunday afternoons for a decade.

"Didn't you used to be Phyllis George?" one woman asked recently. I had to laugh out loud. *I* know that my television personality was just *one* part of my life, but I guess some people don't understand that.

Now, since I'm living in New York again, people have asked me all kinds of questions. "Where have you been? We've missed you!" they say. "What have you been doing?"

When I look back over my fifty-three years, I can confidently say that I was *always* doing something—whether it was in the public eye or not! In fact, it amazes me when I think of the incredible experiences I've had and the different hats I've worn. A friend said to me recently, "Phyllis, if I didn't know better, I'd think you were a ninety-year-old woman with all the things you've done."

It's true. This small-town girl from Texas has been quite busy. Growing up in Denton with my loving parents, Bob and Louise, and my younger brother, Rob, I learned strong, solid values that have seen me through the highs and lows of my professional and personal life to this day.

From the outside, my life may have looked easy—even glamorous at times. But ask any hard-working person and they will assure you that the "ups" always come with the "downs" and the successes are usually paired with the challenges. Like most of you, I've had a healthy dose of both.

One of my friends said, "But Phyllis, with all that you've done I can't imagine anyone has ever told you that you *couldn't* do something. If you write a book on this subject, *no one will believe you!*"

She couldn't have been more wrong. In fact, many times in my life I've heard the words "never" and "can't" from one person or another.

"You'll never win Miss America. You're just a 'bouncy-assed' piano player!"

"You may be Miss America, but you'll never make it in the Big Apple."

"Phyllis, you'll never be a sportscaster. You can't interview superstar athletes. That's a man's job!"

"You can't be the First Lady of Kentucky AND co-host the NFL Today show in New York. What are you thinking?"

"You're getting into the chicken business? What do you know about business, much less chicken?"

"You're going to be in a movie? You've never acted before!"

My personal list of "nevers" is as long and wide as a football field. But somewhere around the fifty-yard line, I stopped paying attention to them. Underneath my outgoing exterior (yes, I *was* named Miss Congeniality in the Miss Texas competition!), I guess you might say I've been quietly driven. I've never been one to let grass grow under my feet for too long. I thrive on challenges and new adventures.

"Where did you get all this energy and drive?" my mother always asked me. I have no idea. I only know I've always been an explorer at heart. I've taught myself to listen to my inner voice: "Go ahead and try it! You can do it! What have you got to lose?" During tough times that inner voice was sometimes a little timid as well. That's when I had to bolster it a bit and say out loud: "Don't you dare give up!" Because often in life, we are the ones standing in our own way.

My spiritual mentor in life was Dr. Norman Vincent Peale, who taught millions of Americans the power of positive thinking. Through his inspirational messages in his bestselling book *The Power of Positive Thinking* (celebrating its fiftieth anniversary this year), his book became the granddaddy of self-help books and is considered by many to have launched the genre. The book and his words are timeless.

"Every time you have a negative thought," Dr. Peale used to say, "push it out and put a positive one in its place." It's simple but profound—and it works. If you do it often enough, soon the positive thoughts become automatic. It's so much easier to be negative, cynical, and jealous. It takes a secure, confident person to be positive. And when you work at keeping a positive attitude, you'll be amazed at the outcome.

I'm writing this book to share with you exactly how I've learned to do that. I found it meant saying yes to yourself; ignoring the nay-sayers; going with the flow of change; knowing when to move on; valuing your special talents; not taking yourself too seriously; and understanding that there is no such thing as failure—only another lesson learned.

All the lessons I've learned in life interweave like pieces of a patchwork quilt. Maybe it's a crazy quilt where the pieces don't match up perfectly. But they are sewn together in a way that makes it a whole because the threads are stories from my life.

Now, I'm no expert at giving advice. But I've led a full and diverse life that has been exciting, exhausting, exasperating, and exhilarating. I have transitioned from one phase to the next, taking the lessons I've learned with me each step of the way. Everything I've learned has been through trial and error. And believe me, I've had some disappointments and made plenty of errors—a few of them doozies. My kids can tell you all about them because I've recounted them over and over for their benefit. I can see them now, rolling their eyes: "Oh, *Mmommm*, you're not going to tell us another *life lesson*, are you?!"

I'm forever bombarding my son, Lincoln, and daughter, Pamela, with nuggets of tried and true wisdom, and I assume they go in one ear and out the other. But one day, out of the blue, Lincoln thanked me for teaching him to treat everyone equally and with respect. Another time I overheard Pamela talking to a friend on the phone, giving advice that I'd passed on to her: "You gotta stay positive ... when you're upbeat, people want to be around you."

And I just have to smile. My words are getting through. Another lesson learned. Parents: keep talking. Your kids may not act like they're listening, but it is sinking in.

I consider myself—and my friends whom you'll meet in this book—life experts. When I mentioned I was writing about the times I had been told "never," suddenly it seemed that everyone had a story to share. Whether these friends came from sports, news, business, entertainment, publishing, the media, or politics, they had all come up against similar obstacles and pushed their way through to success.

So in these chapters, you will also read the "never say never" stories of many of my wonderful friends. We'll start with Muhammad Ali, Larry King, Liz Smith, Roger Staubach, and Chris Evert. Then move on to New York Mayor Michael Bloomberg, Elaine Kaufman, Jane Rosenthal, Richard Kirshenbaum, former Gov. Ann Richards, and Walter Cronkite. Next come Sen. Mary Landrieu, Cathie Black, Barbara Taylor Bradford, Mary Hart, and Walter Anderson. Then you'll hear from Johnny Bench, Kathie Lee Gifford, Irv Cross, Rick Pitino, Reverend Mary Grace Williams, and Paula Zahn. Their experiences have taught me and inspired me, and I know they will do the same for you.

Working on this book has also been an emotional catharsis for me. This past winter on a snowy day, I sat on the cold, concrete floor of a storage unit in Lexington, Kentucky, and opened up box after box that I hadn't gone through in years. Leafing through press clippings, letters, and pictures, I often paused for a tear or a laugh—my life spread out before me. I realized that while I've been fiercely private all these years, I didn't want to keep everything hidden away in those dusty old boxes anymore.

So in this book, I've opened up a few boxes, and I know I've emerged stronger than ever. As you read these ten lessons, some may resonate with you more than others. But I hope these stories motivate you to move forward in your own life. I challenge you to join me in saying "never say never."

1

SAY YES TO YOURSELF

You'll never do it! I'll never do it! Has anyone ever told you that you couldn't do something? Have you ever told yourself you would never do something? If so, you're not alone. Throughout this book you're going to read stories about times some of my friends and I confronted the word "never" and how we overcame it, sometimes with difficulty, to become well known in our various fields.

In this chapter alone, you'll hear from "the Greatest"— Muhammad Ali, CNN talk show king Larry King, and America's favorite gossip columnist, Liz Smith. Plus, you'll learn how my interviews with star athletes Roger Staubach and Dave Cowens helped me create a different style of sportscasting. And you'll see how entering a local beauty pageant after saying I'd *never* do it again gave my life a whole new direction. Ali, Larry, Liz, Roger, Dave, and I have taken different roads to our various successes, but what we share is our strong belief, earned through experience, that **learning to never say never begins with saying yes to yourself.**

What's the problem with "never"? It keeps you from trying. It ensures that you will fail. End of story. "Never" slams doors in your face and pushes away potential opportunities. To be one small voice crying yes in a wilderness of no's is incredibly hard. But I am here to tell you this: To take that first step toward everything you want, everything you can be in life, you must find and nurture in yourself the strength to say yes to yourself, even when others say no.

Banish the words "I can't" from your vocabulary. Remember: If can't equals won't, can equals will.

My unanticipated success as a sportscaster is a perfect example of the importance of saying yes to yourself, even when you are uncertain. It was in 1974, when television sports was dominated by men, that CBS Sports offered me a job. The network executives had seen me cohosting *Candid Camera* with Allen Funt and the Miss America pageant with Bert Parks and liked what they saw. I was building momentum with TV audiences. They could see I had potential and thought they'd take a chance with me. My agent arranged a meeting with Bob Wussler, then vice president of CBS Sports, to explore broadcasting possibilities. Bob explained that he really wanted this to work and that we would have to approach this in a serious way. When CBS offered me a thirteen-week option, they still hadn't determined what role I would play.

Sportscasting? I thought. "Thanks for the offer," I *could* have said, "but I can't do that. I don't know how." Though I'd always been a sports fan, I was not an athlete or an expert; in fact, I had no professional experience in the sports world. Plus, there were no role models for me to emulate. The only female sportscasters at that time were either at local television stations or in temporary slots at the national level. Even my friends were skeptical about whether I could pull it off. A male friend said to me, "Sportscasting is a man's job. It'll never work." *Thanks for the encouragement*, I thought.

Somehow, in the middle of all these uncertainties, I decided to accept the offer. Partly because I needed a job—always an excellent motivator!—and partly because something inside told me I could do it. I had little evidence to support this instinct, but I knew it was at least worth a try.

My first major assignment was an interview with superstar basketball center Dave Cowens of the Boston Celtics. The challenge? To get Cowens—a towering man with a shock of red hair and a reserved nature—to talk to me. The problem? Cowens disliked interviews and had reluctantly agreed to the CBS request because the team management insisted it was good PR. The second problem? He had no idea they were going to send a woman to do the job.

When I arrived at the Celtics' practice with the producer and camera crew in tow, Cowens and his teammates took one look at me and rolled their eyes. I could feel them thinking, "Oh, God. They sent a *girl*?" I tried to ignore them.

"Hey, Dave, how are you?" I cheerily called out to him from courtside. No answer. I tried a second time. Silence. Obviously, Dave was a man of few words. But it just so happened I was a woman of many, *many* words.

As soon as practice was over, Cowens made a beeline for his jeep. I followed, and my producer urged me to hop in. I did. My career was on the line, and I had no intention of going back to New York without talking with him. I'm not going away, I thought to myself. I am getting this interview! So off we went to his log cabin on the outskirts of Boston. The crew trailed behind in the equipment van.

As he drove, Dave stared straight ahead and didn't pay much attention to me. How was I going to get this man to talk? I remembered that my dad had always told me: "Phyllis, you could make a wooden man talk!" Now was the time to test his theory.

For the next forty-five minutes I made comments on anything and everything I could think of: "Wow, it's cold outside! I love your jeep! So what's your cabin like? Where do you go around here on your time off?" I'm the kind of person who gets nervous when I hear silence in a conversation, so I kept talking and talking even though he answered only in monosyllables. This was, of course, before I learned the "art of the pause" in an interview: Sometimes silence leaves space for the most revealing answers.

My experiment in wearing Dave down must have worked, however, because when we reached his cabin, we went into the kitchen. He took a can of beer from the refrigerator and offered me one, which I declined. We settled into rocking chairs on the front porch, he opened his beer, and then he started opening up to me. As I slowly drew him out, we began to have more of a conversation than an interview. He took a few sips of beer. He rocked back and forth in his old chair. And he talked and talked. As the camera rolled, I instinctively tossed aside my formal questions and talked to him like a regular human being, not like a superstar. Mostly I asked him what I was interested to know as a curious fan, questions like: What would you do if it were all over tomorrow? Are there some days you just don't want to suit up? What if you had an injury? Where would you go, what would you do? Do you ever want to settle down and get married?

These were questions that felt natural to me, but I knew no male interviewer had asked an athlete things like this, at least not on camera. It was unheard of to talk about feelings rather than game strategy and statistics, but I knew we could always add that with voice-over later. Getting him to open up like this could come only in a personal conversation. It was not standard procedure, but it felt right.

When we edited the tape to prepare our segment, I knew this was not the Dave Cowens I had seen at practice. Nor was it the Dave Cowens I'd read about. This was the private Dave Cowens underneath the basketball star image. *What would people think?*

The answer came when the interview aired at halftime of the following week's NBA game and the CBS switchboard lit up like a Christmas tree. "We've never seen Cowens like that!" fans raved. "And who was that woman asking him those personal questions?" I was astounded by the overwhelmingly positive response.

The producers realized something new and distinctive was happening. I had gotten a sports star to remove his armor, and the fans ate it up. By doing that I had discovered my special talent: disarming a stubborn interview subject and convincing him to reveal himself to a television audience. My producers and I knew that no one else was covering sports from the human interest angle. I went for the heart, and the athletes gave heart back. By saying yes, I can, and then doing it I opened up a new opportunity for sports broadcasting and myself.

The interviews were so successful, in fact, that CBS signed me to a three-year deal. And soon they assigned me to cohost their new show, *The NFL Today*, a pregame football program on Sunday afternoons. On that show I talked football with my cohosts and also worked on human interest stories about the superstar players. *The NFL Today* team consisted of veteran sportscaster Brent Musberger; Irv Cross, a former player for the Philadelphia Eagles (whom you'll read more about in Chapter 8); and me. We had such good chemistry that we were dubbed "the Mod Squad of CBS Sports." Brent, Irv, and I enjoyed it so much that our enthusiasm came across as genuine and spontaneous. Each of us had a role. Brent was the traffic cop. He called on us and tied it all together. Irv talked about stats and strategies, and I interviewed the players. Bob Wussler deserves all the credit for putting our team together. Bob was a mentor and friend. His support and encouragement helped me be myself and were key to my success.

Over the ten happy years I was at CBS Sports, my interviews were known for my willingness to ask athletes what others wouldn't. Often I used my gut instinct to ask the questions and get the answers I thought the audience wanted to hear. Sometimes the interviewees said things that surprised even them.

One of my best-known interviews was with superstar Dallas Cowboys quarterback Roger Staubach (whom you'll read more about in Chapter 2). Since I grew up in Texas, the Cowboys were always my favorite team. Roger was one of the greatest quarterbacks ever, known for leading his team to dramatic comeback victories. But he also had a reputation as a straitlaced, squeaky-clean guy. A graduate of the U.S. Naval Academy, he'd served in the Navy before turning pro, and people said he was a devout Catholic.

When I interviewed Roger, I wanted to dig beneath that image. After I asked him some football questions, I got more personal.

"You know, Roger," I began, "everybody knows you as the all-American guy with a straight, square image. Do you ever get tired of that?"

"Well, Phyllis," he said, looking me straight in the eye, "well, yes. I have a station wagon, and I put the kids in the back, and we all go to church every Sunday. But," he said, clearing his throat, *"let me tell you:* I like sex just as much as Joe Namath. Only I like it with one person—my wife, Marianne!"

I blinked hard and smiled as my voice went up an octave. I caught Marianne out of the corner of my eye blushing as she dashed from the house.

When the interview ran, the CBS switchboard flashed like a pinball machine. Plus, the story made headlines in newspaper sports sections and celebrity gossip columns all around the country. Roger Staubach talking about his *sex life* and comparing himself to the playboy Broadway Joe Namath—that was news! To this day, Roger tells this story in all his speeches.

Interviews like that became one of the hallmarks of our show. We brought the athletes out from behind their helmets and shoulder pads and gave them a face and a personality. We made them real to the fans. A little over a year later, I was on the cover of *People* magazine with the title "the First Lady of the Locker Room." Our Emmy Award–winning show had become an instant hit. That half-hour pregame show—which was really only twenty-four minutes since six minutes were for commercials—made us household names. There were stories about people going to church early so they could be home in time to watch. In 2001 Rudy Martzke, *USA Today*'s sports television critic, called us "perhaps the most popular sports studio team in history." Even today people tell me how much they loved the show and ask why we don't do it again.

Lesson: Saying yes to yourself opens up opportunities that can take you anywhere. Having a mentor in your life who says yes to you is also key. Appreciate your mentors when you're starting out. And later, always give credit to the people who were there with you at the beginning.

Having a can-do spirit and a mentor who believed in him also took my friend Larry King from being a little boy with a dream to becoming one of our most popular and powerful broadcasters. His *Larry King Live* on CNN sets the standard for insightful one-on-one conversations with newsmakers of the day. Since debuting on CNN in 1985, he has conducted more than 40,000 interviews; received multiple Emmy, George Foster Peabody, and CableACE awards; and published twelve books.

Larry wanted to be a broadcaster from the time he was five years old. "One of my earliest memories," he told me, "is staring at the radio and wanting to be an announcer. Through my teen years, all my friends would laugh and make fun of the fact that at baseball games I would roll up a scorecard, pretend it was a microphone, and proceed to broadcast the game to myself."

But his dreams had to be put on hold when Larry's father died when he was nine and a half years old and he had to help his mother out until his brother finished school. After high school, Larry says, "I knocked around at a bunch of odd jobs, always wishing to someday break into radio and then, hopefully, television."

Finally, at age twenty-two and a half he took a train to Miami and arrived with $13 in his pocket. "I was staying at my uncle's small apartment," Larry remembers, "and I went around all day from station to station auditioning and being turned down—until I walked into a small radio station at the southernmost tip of Miami Beach called WAHR."

Larry credits the late Marshall Simmonds as his "savior in life." Simmonds listened to his tape and told him, "'Kid, the next opening we have, I'm going to give you a chance.' That chance occurred on May 1, 1957. Marshall would give me my name, all the encouragement in the world, and the drive to make it."

Simmonds also gave Larry the advice he has followed his entire career. "'The only secret in the business,'" he remembers Simmonds telling him, "'is that there is no secret. Just be yourself. If the people like it, they will like it. And if they don't, they won't.' It really is as simple as that, and I have not forgotten that to this day."

Just be yourself. You will gain confidence by accepting yourself as you are and being true to yourself in all that you do. After accepting yourself, build confidence by taking responsibility for whatever challenges come your way.

Liz Smith learned that lesson in one of her early jobs and has used it to become one of the most widely read columnists in America. Her daily gossip column about celebrities is syndicated nationally to millions of eager readers in over seventy newspapers, and she's known as one of the highest-paid female print journalists in the world. In her autobiography, *Natural Blonde*, she used her wonderful wit to describe growing up in rural Texas and her subsequent years in New York—from her early success in print and broadcast journalism to the present. A fellow Texan, Liz befriended me when I first moved to New York shortly after being Miss America. She is one of the most civic-minded people I know. I am constantly amazed by her knowledge of what's going on, who's doing it, and what everybody is saying about it.

But a lot of people don't realize that Liz started out as a pioneer woman in television's early years when she first moved to New York in 1949. "Back in the fifties," she says, "when TV was still young, cameras were bigger than refrigerators, there were no satellites to send signals by, and everything was black and white. I worked as a field producer for a live show called *Wide Wide World*."

The challenges in those days were many. "We were constantly asked to make bricks with straw, to perform miracles, to convince large organizations to change the dates of events so we could film them live on Sunday morning," she says. "All the NBC producers were interested in was *results*."

As a young woman in a new career, Liz was in an especially tenuous position. "Because so much was demanded of us," she recalls, "I discovered that I had developed a habit of taking a problem now and then back to the boss, laying it at his feet, and saying, 'It can't be done.' I was shocked also to realize that because I was a woman and women then had no status or clout, I rather enjoyed putting the problem back in the lap of some overpaid guy who wanted me to do the impossible."

But soon Liz had a breakthrough insight that helped her become the success she is today. "Once I realized what I was doing, I couldn't do it any longer," she says. "My sense of what was right no longer enjoyed the petty little triumph. I decided then not to present people with problems. I started to become a part of the solution instead of a part of the problem. I began to accomplish more miracles and pull off more impossible stories, and I became one of the line producers everybody wanted to work with."

Liz discovered that changing "no, I can't" to "yes, I can" transformed her into a self-starter who took responsibility for solving problems on her own and became a key to her success. She eventually left TV production and went into print journalism, but she says, "I never forgot the triumph of that lesson."

Be a self-starter. When an impossible challenge comes your way, recognize it and seize it. Whether it's a challenge or a problem, take ownership of it and solve it. View it as an opportunity to shine. Becoming a problem-solver will build your reputation among others and your confidence in yourself. The feeling of doing so will be exhilarating.

~

One of the first impossible challenges I seized occurred not in the fast lane of television but in the perhaps equally competitive land of beauty pageants. Hey, everybody's got to start somewhere! Being Miss America was a great honor and a springboard for me into the rest of my life. Getting there was also an adventure that taught me important lessons about saying yes to myself.

It all goes back to one persistent pageant official who got me over my first big "never." Until then I had lived in a world of "yes," growing up in a solid, loving family in the small town of Denton, Texas, between Dallas and Fort Worth. In high school I was a cheerleader, appeared in school plays, and had lots of friends and a steady boyfriend. I was president of the junior class as well as president of the Methodist Youth Fellowship. After fourteen years of classical training under the guidance of the internationally known concert pianist Dr. Isabel Scionti, I could play the piano like nobody's business. When you put it all together, I was very happy in life. The few times I was told "no" or "never" had to do with not putting my elbows on the dinner table, not gossiping about the neighbors, not horsing around with my younger brother, or not wearing my skirts too short.

When I was eighteen, the local Jaycees encouraged me to enter the Miss Denton pageant. I entered, and much to my surprise, I won. "Well," I thought, "that wasn't so hard!" Beauty queen–dom might open up some new opportunities for this small-town girl.

As Miss Denton, my next step was the Miss Texas pageant. One month later, there I was on stage again, and I was surprised to win all the categories of swimsuit, evening gown, talent, and even Miss Congeniality. I could feel the audience rooting for me; I was told that the press even thought I'd be crowned Miss Texas. On the final night of the competition, the *Fort Worth Star-Telegram* had already laid out the front page with my picture on it—just without the headline.

And then ... the winners were announced. I was named second runner-up! I was crushed. It was my first big disappointment. I went home and sat around, licking my wounds and trying to figure out what I had done wrong. It was especially dispiriting because people kept telling me I should have won. But when I found no answers, my next step was to give up. I decided that I would never enter another pageant as long as I lived. Who needs it? Why try so hard and come so close, only to feel like a failure? Remember how it felt when you didn't get the prom date you wanted? Or when you were passed over for a role in the school play? Or when you were not chosen for the varsity team when you were convinced you were ready? There's something about those early disappointments that stays with us the rest of our lives—even though we always learn from them.

Now I know that incident did teach me an important lesson: *Sometimes you do the best you can and still lose. You can't always come in first, since there are circumstances beyond your control, and you can't take it personally.* I wasn't interested in learning from it at the time, however. I simply refused to try again. But someone else felt differently. Soon an official from the Miss Dallas pageant started telephoning me, urging me to enter the next year's competition. I spent a lot of time in Dallas because I was in commercials and modeling there while attending the University of North Texas in Denton as an education and speech major.

"I really think you can win it," he insisted. "You've got to give it a chance." I gave him my prepared "never" speech. No way was I going to set myself up for failure again. But he kept calling. He left messages with my parents, emphasizing the scholarship money I would receive if I entered and won. I kept saying to myself and to him, "No, never!" By that time, I had started student-teaching in an elementary school, and I had a steady boyfriend. This competition seemed like a distraction, not an opportunity.

Then, a few months later, I came home from my sorority house one Friday night to do my laundry. It was close to midnight, and as I came up the front porch steps struggling with my dirty clothes, I could hear the phone ringing off the hook. This was 1970, remember, a world before answering machines. Dad was asleep on the couch and Mom was still at her weekly bridge game, so I dropped the clothes in the foyer, ran to the kitchen, and answered the phone.

"Phyllis!" said the earnest voice on the other end of the line. "I'm giving this one last shot." It was the official from the Miss Dallas pageant. Clearly *this* was someone who never took no for an answer. "Tomorrow are the preliminaries for Miss Dallas. You've got to be there," he insisted.

I paused. What should I do? I was quiet for a moment, and then I heard that little voice in my head whisper, "Phyllis Ann, just say yes. If this guy is so convinced you have a chance, maybe he's right."

"Okay, all right," I told him. "I'll do it." With that, I was back in the pageant business. After we hung up, I frantically called my mother at her bridge game to break the news. She was stunned after all this time I'd been saying no. Still, she rushed home, and we dug out my evening gown and swimsuit from the year before. I'll admit I had put on a few pounds. Ten, to be exact. Well, I'd just have to think thin.

In the preliminaries the next day I was woefully unprepared. The swimsuit competition revealed how out of shape I was. And in the talent competition I performed the same thing I'd played the previous year, though I'd barely practiced it at all. It was (get ready to be impressed) a Glen Campbell medley, including "Wichita Lineman," played with a classical flair! The truth was that I barely made the finals. I often wonder, if I had not succeeded that night, how my life would have been different. Somehow, though, a few weeks later I was crowned Miss Dallas. With that, I was on my way to Miss Texas and eventually Miss America.

I never really understood why that pageant official was so convinced that I could win. But the combination of his persistence and his belief in me made me think that maybe there was something worth going for.

Listen to the right people. It can help you develop the can-do spirit in yourself. The right person might be someone you have a passing relationship with, as in my case. Or it might be someone who has a major role in your life, like your parents, your teachers and coaches if you're in school, or your supervisors, community leaders, or friends at other times. It might even come out of left field, as a surprise from an unexpected source at a time of need.

I heard Barbara Walters tell a great story at a luncheon this spring sponsored by American Women in Radio and Television honoring the fifty greatest women in radio and television. We think of Walters nowadays as being virtually invincible, one of the most respected journalists, male or female, on television and the trailblazer for women in the field. But at this event she talked about a time when she was feeling besieged. She'd been selected to be the first woman coanchor of a national nightly news program, but the doubters were sniping all around her head—questioning the salary she was earning, her ability to hold an audience, and whether she could cut it.

She was starting to question herself as well when one day a telegram arrived for her at the ABC studio. She ripped it open and read the one sentence it contained: "Don't let the bastards get you down." Signed John Wayne. America's favorite cowboy riding to her defense! This voice of affirmation from a surprise—and unexpected—source helped Walters regain her confidence in herself. And even though she left that position not long afterward on her way to other accomplishments, she never forgot how his support had helped at a crucial moment in her career.

This is important in learning to say yes to yourself because the counterpart of learning to listen to the right people is learning to not listen to the wrong people. In fact, take it a step further. *Use others' doubts to motivate yourself. When others question your ability to accomplish something, prove them wrong.*

My friend Muhammad Ali has been a hero to so many for so long, even when facing the challenges of Parkinson's disease, that it is hard to believe that anyone ever thought this boxing legend and cultural icon couldn't do something.

But Ali counts as a turning point his first bout against Sonny Liston in 1964, "one of the most important fights of my entire career," he says. "It was my first world heavyweight champion title fight, and Liston was my most difficult opponent up to that point. Everyone told me it couldn't be done.

Boxing critics, commentators, people in the street … the odds were not in my favor. 'He can't do it,' they all said. 'There's no way Cassius Clay can beat Sonny Liston.' Cassius Clay will never win."

But Ali (whose name was then Cassius Clay) refused to listen. "I told them they were wrong," he says. "I knew I had a chance. I knew I could beat Sonny Liston."

He had to dig deep during the fight when "the situation became intense. I went on the offensive with jabs and uppercuts. My eyes burned bad in the fifth round. I could see a little, but not much." Ali fell back on the support of someone he knew he could count on. "Angelo Dundee, my trainer, pushed me out of the corner," he says. "He told me to keep going. Don't give up."

Ali proved the doubters wrong. "Before I knew it, the fight was over. Liston was out! I knocked out the man who once reigned over the heavyweight division, and I became the world heavyweight champion. I shook up the world and proved all of my detractors wrong. I told them I was gonna get Liston, and I got him. And in 1965 I got him again, defending my world heavyweight title. And they thought I'd never win!"

~

On my way to becoming Miss America, I encountered a *lightweight* naysayer—but I used his doubts to motivate myself as well.

After winning the Miss Dallas contest, I had begun planning to compete at the Miss Texas pageant. I'd lost the year before. Now, if I was going to compete, I was determined to win. I even had a new piano piece for the talent competition: a popular medley of "Raindrops Keep Falling on My Head" and "Promises, Promises"—*again* played with a classical flair!

Eight weeks later I stood on stage next to sixty of the most beautiful, talented, smart, dynamic women I'd ever met. But this time I was a seasoned veteran. In a strange way, my loss the year before had given me confidence as well as experience. This time instead of letting the past failure push me down, I used it to build me up. Again, I won swimsuit, talent, and evening gown—though not Miss Congeniality! The year before I'd focused on being a people pleaser and having a good time. This year I was still friendly, but now my goals were different: I was determined to win.

And this time the judges voted me Miss Texas for 1970. **Lesson: Try it once, and if it doesn't work, try it again. Learn from your experience. Keep trying until you get it right.**

Next, I prepared to represent Texas in the big one, the Miss America pageant. With just two months to go, I psyched myself up with positive talk: "Stay focused but enjoy the experience. You can do this," I repeated to myself over and over. I'd learned from experience that I needed to be in great shape mentally and physically to project myself the most effectively. I worked hard on getting into great shape: lots of bike riding and swimming and no more French fries (my downfall) at our local hangout, the Sonic. I also boosted my self-confidence by making sure I was up to date on current events and issues, and was prepared to discuss them.

But then I heard what the executive director of the state pageant was telling everyone. "Oh, Phyllis ... she'll *never* win. *She's just a bouncy-assed piano player!*"

That hurt my pride—and more than that, it made me more determined. With my newfound confidence, I turned that negative energy into motivation. "*Bouncy assed*, huh?" I'd think. "I'll show that guy." In just one year's time I had made a vital shift in my way of thinking. I went from "I'll never do that again" to "Watch me do it."

When I arrived in Atlantic City for the pageant, seeing the boardwalk and the convention center was the first thrill. Then came the boardwalk parade and the first three nights of preliminary competition. My family and I had watched the pageant on television for years, and now everything that at one point had seemed larger than life was right in front of me. And I was in it, competing and enjoying it all.

Then the final day of the competition arrived. A group of women from the women's liberation movement were burning their bras on the boardwalk outside Convention Hall. They were proclaiming their independence from social restrictions and protesting that we contestants were being exploited, especially by having to parade around in swimsuits. I had mixed feelings about the protest. Even though I'd won the swimsuit competition, I despised that part of it; most of the other contestants did as well. But in spite of those reservations, I saw the pageant as an opportunity, a way to earn scholarship money and a springboard to new possibilities.

Besides, the bra-burning women weren't the only ones making a statement of independence. That day I was also demonstrating my freedom from the old restrictions that had limited me in the past. "There are two things that can happen today," I told myself. "I can win, and I can win. Even if I don't come in first place, it's not a failure because I learned something important these last few months. I've learned to keep strong on the inside no matter what people say or what happens around me."

That night, on stage, it came down to Miss South Carolina and me. We held each other's hands as Bert Parks, the legendary emcee, made the big announcement. When Bert called my name, my hands flew to my face in shock. I cried, I gasped, I trembled. I did all those things the winners before me had done that I had promised myself I wouldn't do.

The reigning Miss America, Pamela Eldred, put the robe on me—it was a mile long and felt like it weighed a ton—draped the banner around me, and handed me a gold scepter. Then she crowned me the fiftieth Miss America with the pageant's first gold crown. Bert sang the well-known "There she is … Miss America," as I took the walk down the runway. Up to that point, it was the biggest moment in my life.

Okay, it's not like I'd discovered a cure for cancer or written the great American novel. But if I'd gotten this far, who knew what else I could do? And in the course of getting to this point in my life, I'd learned valuable lessons that would continue to guide me throughout. Being Miss America opened a whole world of opportunities to me and catapulted me into the rest of my life. Had I not said yes to that insistent pageant official and yes to myself, I would never have known how far I could go.

Sometimes opportunity arrives when you're taking the dirty laundry home and the phone rings. Answer it. Starting to believe "I can" instead of "I can't" can truly change the course of your life.

Lesson

2

EMBRACE CHANGE
AS YOUR FRIEND

Can you think of all the changes you've experienced in life, both large and small? At last count I've had at least five distinct careers, have lived in four states, and have been married twice. That's a lot of change!

Some people say, "Oh, Phyllis, you keep reinventing yourself." But that's not quite true. It may seem from the outside that I'm constantly choosing new directions, new cities, and new lives. But the changes I've experienced—and continue to experience—are seldom the result of a conscious choice or plan. They are more about finding myself at a crossroads and then choosing the best path to take. When something isn't working for me, I make a change. When something *is* working, I don't assume it will keep working forever. Nothing is forever, so keep moving. The old saying is true: "If you snooze, you lose."

I like to view the changes in my life as natural transitions from one phase to the next. Being Miss America, a sportscaster, a governor's wife, an entrepreneur, and an author may seem unrelated to each other. But each one prepared me for the next and made it more likely I would be successful each time I tried something new.

Sometimes changes are difficult; sometimes they are painful. Sometimes you change but the people around you don't. Don't let that stop you. Encourage them to come along with you, but if they can't, you still have to move forward and hope that they catch up with you.

In spite of the difficulties, any change offers an opportunity for growth, self-improvement, and movement. If you stayed on the same road your entire life trip, it would be boring. At the end of your journey, you'd wonder, "What have I done with my life? I just sat here in this Laz-E-Boy in the same family room eating the same meals and watching the same TV shows day in and day out." Before you know it, life is over. *So get out of that Laz-E-Boy!* What are you afraid of? A lot, you admit. Read on.

~

The first step in dealing with change is to understand it's nothing to be afraid of. Going from being a small-town girl who had seldom left Texas to a Miss America who jetted all over the country was the first huge change in *my* life. The night after winning the title I sat in my Atlantic City hotel room on the boardwalk overlooking the ocean. With all the activity around me, I still felt very lonely and fought the urge to panic. The room was filled with pageant officials I'd met that week, security men, and other people I'd never seen before. I was introduced to my chaperone, who would accompany me 24/7 for the next year. And these strangers had taken over my life! They were now in charge of telling me where to go and what to do.

My family was at another hotel, preparing to drive back to Texas early the next morning. I remember calling my mother that evening. "What have I done?" I gasped. "My whole life has changed!" I already had a travel itinerary for the next day, and the first stop—King of Prussia, Pennsylvania—was a place I'd never heard of. "Honey, it's going to be okay," she soothed me. "It's only for a year." But I knew at that moment my life would never be the same again. I was separated from my family and friends. I was leaving the life I felt secure in, my comfort zone. And that was scary.

The change was immediate and drastic. It was a different city and state every day, a different bed every night, a different group of people to meet and engage in conversation. In every city I met with reporters, shook hundreds of hands, gave hundreds of speeches, and talked with strangers in lobbies, restaurants, and airports. I lived out of two suitcases jam-packed with four dresses, two pantsuits, two cocktail dresses, three evening gowns, six pairs of shoes, and four purses, not to mention toiletries, makeup, hair dryers, and electric curlers. I was constantly "on duty." When I stepped off the plane each day, I had to look like a million bucks, smiling all the way—even if I didn't feel like it.

When you're Miss America, you never get a second chance to make a first impression. Everyone wanted to see up close what a Miss America looked like: what I was wearing, which color nail polish I used, whether I wore false eyelashes, how I was styling my hair. I was inspected to make sure I was a fitting representative of this American institution. It's an experience all Miss Americas have shared.

At the end of each day I'd drop into bed exhausted. Some nights I barely had the energy to wipe off my makeup or take off my clothes. I fell into bed and went right to sleep. The schedule was grueling, and at first I didn't know how I was going to cope.

But after the first month I started to realize that *while change can seem frightening, it's necessary for growth*. I told myself, "This is a job. I have a one-year contract. I'm going to fulfill that contract and do my best. I can do this." And once I relaxed a bit, I began to see how this change was opening up a whole new world of opportunities for me. I traveled to places, met people, and had experiences I would never have had otherwise. Before then I was living a happy existence in Denton, Texas, thinking I knew everything about myself and what I wanted. But venturing out of my small world, I realized I was just a little pea in the grand scheme of things and maybe I didn't know so much after all. This change gave me the opportunity to open my eyes and see that the pie was a lot bigger than I thought—and so was the piece I wanted.

Some of the challenges were bigger than others. Just before leaving on a trip to St. Louis, I was told that a threat had been made on my life and a sky marshal had to travel with me. I was terrified, wondering if some deranged man with a gun would be waiting when we arrived. Al Marks, then executive director of the Miss America pageant, calmed me by saying he knew I was scared, but I couldn't let fear dominate my actions. So I made the trip. When we landed, I took a deep breath, stepped off the plane, and walked over to the fence to shake the hands of the people there to meet me. When it was over, I got into my waiting car and finally exhaled.

At the end of that year I felt I'd earned a Ph.D. in human relations. Without the protection of my family and friends around me, I'd learned how to deal with people in all kinds of situations and how to take care of myself.

In a new situation you discover your strengths. When the safety net is pulled away, there is always an initial fear that you will fall. Most people have this feeling. But it is a time to find out what strengths you have deep within. Believe they are there.

A year later—*boom!*—another big change. Amid streaming tears and swelling music, I crowned the new Miss America, Laurie Lee Schaffer. As the spotlight shifted to her, the lights went out for me. As quickly as they giveth, they taketh away! Suddenly I was no longer this identity I had lived with and finally gotten comfortable with all year. I was no longer the center of attention. After twelve months of schedules and speeches and every minute accounted for, I now had no idea what to do with myself. Where do I go, what do I do? Where did everybody go? Nobody's calling! Doesn't anyone care anymore?

First I went home to Denton and slept. I was exhausted. I spent a week on the couch at my parents' home watching TV in dazed despair. In between game shows, I'd stare out the sliding glass doors that led to the patio in the backyard. When I finally snapped out of it, my life became somewhat normal again. Though there isn't really a "back to normal" once you've been a Miss America. I could win an Oscar or travel to the moon or become president, but I will always be introduced as "the former Miss America."

The previous year had taught me not to fear change when it brought a new beginning. Now I had to learn to accept change when it brought an ending—and to use what I'd learned to begin again. I decided to move to Dallas and share an apartment with two sorority sisters. If at first I worried what I would do, my concerns soon vanished. I was booked for speaking engagements and emceeing weeklong state pageants around the country. I began having a social life once again, and professional opportunities started coming my way.

I needed that transition year to readjust, refocus, recharge, and refuel. But after that I wanted to launch myself into a career in broadcasting or the entertainment industry. What I really wanted to do was move to New York—the Big Apple! I knew it would be a tremendous change, but now I felt I could handle it.

Of course, I had visited New York many times as Miss America, but moving there to live was another story. Talk about another drastic change! Everything was different from what I knew growing up: the energy level, the traffic, the cultural diversity, the cabs racing from the West Side to the East Side, north to south, the in-your-face lifestyle, the *noise*.

Other Miss Americas had tried to make it here and decided it wasn't for them, and soon I began to see what we were up against. I was proud of my title and of being part of a tradition that has survived the Depression, war, scandal, and social movements. But in New York people were tougher on me *because* I had been Miss America. I'd go on auditions for commercials ("go-sees," they were called), and casting directors would say, "*So*, you were Miss America," looking me up and down. I discovered my first challenge was to alter whatever preconceived notion they had of "a Miss America." Sometimes that line on my résumé got me in the door. People would say, "Yeah, bring her in." But once I got in, they made it clear it was no advantage having once worn a crown. I was told by many casting agents, "You're just another pretty face in a sea of pretty faces."

It was another change to a new life that called for an adjustment. I had a healthy sense of confidence in myself, but after the first month I wondered, Is this really worth it? How am I going to prove myself in this new arena? I kept remembering this guy who said to me, "You may be Miss America, but you'll never make it in the Big Apple." Maybe I *should* go back home....

It took a while, but I knew if I didn't want to leave, I had to make it work. I got very competitive. I redoubled my efforts, kept learning all I could, and repeated again and again to myself that I was not going to give up so easily. "You can do it, Phyllis!" I repeated to myself. And pretty soon my acting lessons started to lead to work in television commercials. I did ads for Woolite, Oster blenders, Close-up toothpaste, and Cotton Incorporated. I looked into a freshly washed plate in an ad for Joy dishwashing liquid and said, "It's so clear, I can even see myself!" I dived off a diving board in a Playtex bra under my tight turtleneck sweater, and when I came up, I looked into the camera on the side of the pool and said, "See? It *still* looks good. Even wet. A Playtex bra always keeps its shape."

All that led to my first big television break when I was chosen as the first cohost for Allen Funt on *Candid Camera*. And before too long I heard them saying, "Phyllis isn't just another pretty face...." I was surviving, and I was on my way.

More than a decade after I finished my Miss America term, I had a déjà vu, though I was better prepared this time. After a busy four years as governor of Kentucky, my former husband John's term was over, and so was my reign as first lady. Everything stopped at midnight. "When you wake up tomorrow," John said on our last night at the mansion, "and you punch zero on the phone, you're not going to get the state trooper anymore. You're going to get the downtown operator just like everyone else."

Such huge, dramatic changes can leave you feeling hollow inside because your comfort zone is gone. Once again, all of a sudden I had no schedule and no meetings, nobody was calling, and I wasn't running late for anything. I wondered: What are we going to do? Where are we going? Still, I had my two beautiful children, Lincoln and Pamela, to keep me busy. And I somehow knew that although it would be a big adjustment, I could make it just as I'd done before.

New beginnings will lead to new endings, and the cycle will start all over again. So accept change. It is part of the natural order of life. Each time you go through change you'll be stronger and have greater confidence for the next time around.

~

You know Roger Staubach as a Heisman Trophy winner and Hall of Fame quarterback of the Dallas Cowboys, but he is also an expert on change. Roger and I met when I interviewed him on *The NFL Today* on CBS, and we have stayed in touch ever since. As a result of having to learn how to accept change, he says today that "life is all about transitions and moving forward."

Considering that Roger is one of the greatest quarterbacks ever to have played the game, it's amazing how close he came to never being a quarterback at all. He spent most of his high school years playing running back. "But our head coach changed my life because one day he said to me, 'I want you to be quarterback.' It was my senior year, and he just switched me," Roger remembers. "I didn't want to be a quarterback. But the coach said, 'The reason I want you to be quarterback is because the other guys will listen to you.' So I did it and I worked hard at it." From that experience, Roger learned not to be afraid of change because sometimes changes you initially don't want to make can work out for the best: "If you take on something new, you've got to use what you have and do it to the best of your ability."

"That lesson was instrumental to me years later, when I left the service and wanted to go back to football," he says. After Roger's graduation from the U.S. Naval Academy, he served his obligatory four years in the Navy, including one year in Vietnam. Although he'd been a college star, no one expected that he could return after that and become a pro.

"People said, 'Well, you can't be away for four years and then come back and play quarterback again! After four years? No way,'" he says. "I started to think, Well, maybe that's true. And each year I was in the service, I was thinking I'd never play again. Then I just made up my mind: Hey, if I can play at age twenty-three, I should be able to play at age twenty-seven. What's the difference?"

Once Roger made up his mind, he faced a tough road back. "There weren't any examples out there of someone else who had done this," he says. "If I hadn't had this never say never type of thinking and listened to those around me, maybe I would have lost confidence and I wouldn't have worked out as hard. But I didn't want to do what people thought I was going to do—which was to fail. When I trained, I really pushed myself. I figured if I pushed myself, that was all I could do. And if I pushed myself, it would give me the confidence I needed to be successful."

And he did it. He entered the NFL as a rookie with the Cowboys at twenty-seven. He went on to play for eleven years, leading the team to four NFC titles and two Super Bowl championships.

After achieving success against the odds in the NFL, Roger then faced another challenging transition when he retired from football at age thirty-eight. "I had worked in the off-season in real estate," he says, "so when I got out of football, I knew I could give real estate a shot. But I had trained all my life to be a professional athlete. I couldn't then just take what I learned there into the next arena. I had to get the experience and dedicate the time to this new venture, too. It's that never say never attitude again."

Roger was realistic about what it took to establish himself in a new profession. "I didn't walk out and say, 'Hey, I'm a big shot … here I am.' A lot of the customers I called up would say to me, 'Roger, I'm sure you're a nice guy and that was a great game you played, but what do you know about real estate?' However, once they saw that I had committed myself to it, I was in business."

Today Roger's commercial real estate company, the Staubach Company, has offices in Dallas, New York, and seventeen other U.S. cities and partnerships around the world. The twenty-five-year-old company is one of the nation's largest full-service tenant representation firms. Its clients include some of the biggest names in American business.

Roger's ability to change has resulted in success in each stage of his life. "I believe in moving forward," he says. "I love that old saying: *'There's no traffic jam in the extra mile.'*"

Roger's extra efforts to become a rookie at age twenty-seven are unusual since most athletes do not turn pro that late in their lives. But being attuned to their own physical and mental abilities is one reason professional athletes can adapt to change over the course of their playing careers.

Tennis legend Chris Evert is an all-star athlete whom I first met as a sportscaster. Over the course of her twenty-year career she gained everyone's admiration for her ability to remain competitive for so long. She won at least one grand slam singles title every year from 1974 to 1986. At her retirement in 1989, she had won 157 pro singles titles and 18 majors titles. Part of her success is due to her acceptance of change and her ability to discover new strengths to keep challenging her opponents.

"I remember at age thirty at the beginning of the tennis year, an analyst said that I was past my prime and I could not win a grand slam ever again," she says. "My ego was crushed, but it made me more determined and gave me more incentive."

Not only did Chrissy use others' doubts to motivate her—always a key aspect of success—she learned how to use the advantages of her age. "That year I beat Martina Navratilova in the French final," she remembers. "I attributed that win to many years of experience and knowledge and the fact that I paced myself. All three went hand in hand."

"While the younger players could train harder and stay out there longer," she says, "I was smart enough to realize that I had to pack a lot into a shorter amount of time. Also, even though a few losses to younger players were starting to take away some of my confidence, I still felt that if I hung in there, I could mentally outlast them."

~

We admire people like Roger and Chris who accept and make the best of the changes that come with age, retirement, and the end of one phase in life and the beginning of another. But we must also be prepared for those times when a change to something we thought we wanted doesn't work out.

In 1977, when I married my first husband, the famous film producer Robert Evans (best known for *The Godfather*, *Love Story*, and *Chinatown*), he was at the height of his career. Although I'd traveled to Los Angeles frequently to do sports interviews, I'd never imagined myself living in Beverly Hills. Once again, I entered a whole new world where I was the stranger in a strange land: Hollywood!

Bob had seen me on the cover of *People* magazine and, through mutual friends, had arranged a meeting. It was shortly after I had ended a serious five-year relationship, and I was still vulnerable. He was worldly with great style; I was ready to be swept off my feet. We married very soon after meeting, and I moved into his beautiful mansion. However, I kept my apartment in New York City since I was still flying coast to coast for my job on *The NFL Today* show.

As Bob's wife, I experienced Hollywood firsthand and close up. It was like living in a movie. In the morning the butler would bring us breakfast by the pool. Then I'd play a little tennis on our court. Stars would drop by for an afternoon visit or for dinner and a screening: Warren Beatty, Jack Nicholson, Kirk Douglas, Dustin Hoffman, and others. Most days, our house was a beautiful set with these beautiful people milling about. That life continued when we traveled as well. There were trips to the famous Hotel du Cap in the south of France and to the international film festival in Taormina, Sicily. In Acapulco we socialized with Natalie Wood and Robert Wagner, who happened to be there as well.

For all the excitement, though, some aspects of Bob's larger-than-life world were uncomfortable for me from the start. In Hollywood you had to keep up the perception that you were successful, that you had big projects in development, that you were *always* working. If you didn't have a highly rated sitcom or movie of the week or box office hit, you were yesterday's news. There was no resting on your laurels in that town.

I was accustomed to working in the high-stakes, high-pressure television world of New York, so I was hardly naive. But

Hollywood was a company town, and I always felt like an observer, on the outside looking in, and not really a part of it. I never felt grounded. At a later stage in my life, it would have been very different and I would have been comfortable living in LA. Now, in fact, I've established wonderful friendships and made great business contacts and always enjoy my trips there. But at that point it wasn't right for me.

I also realized that Bob and I had jumped into marriage too quickly, before we really knew each other. I tried to adapt, but *when you try to be something you're not, it never works*. In his autobiography Bob said that my idea of marriage was a big white house, children, and church on Sunday. He was right, and later I would have that in Kentucky. But I knew Hollywood was not a place I wanted to grow old in. Our whirlwind marriage ended after eleven months, though Bob and I had an amicable split. Thank God I had kept my New York apartment and my job in sportscasting, and so I could move back to a place that was a better fit for me. As my friend Kenny Rogers sings, "You've gotta know when to hold 'em, know when to fold 'em."

Sometimes you make a change and it's not right for you. Recognize it, deal with it, and move forward. Understand that those changes are useful, too, because from them you learn what you don't want or don't need. Leaving something that's not right is not moving backward. It's a step closer to a more compatible setting where you can use what you've learned.

≈

Change is inevitable and nothing to be afraid of. After twenty years of living in Kentucky, here I am in New York starting over again. I left peaceful Kentucky and returned to the frenzied pace of New York City. I went from my 175-year-old, seventeen-acre estate, Cave Hill Place, to a two-bedroom Fifth Avenue apartment. Instead of overlooking the rolling bluegrass of Kentucky, I now have Central Park as my front yard. I cut my big hair, got rid of a lot of my colorful clothes, and started to dress in black and gray like other New Yorkers. It was again a major life change, but this time I was wiser about starting over.

Change can be rocky and unsettling. It can make you feel insecure and off balance. But change always makes you stronger, more in control of yourself, more exciting, more interesting.

Now change to me is like an old friend. I know it's not my enemy anymore. And I know it will keep coming back to visit again and again to teach me something new.

3

BE A RISK TAKER

What do a billionaire, a restaurateur, a movie producer, and a former first lady have in common? They've taken to heart Ralph Waldo Emerson's words: "Do not go where the path may lead; go instead where there is no path and leave a trail." These are the risk takers you'll meet in this chapter.

Throughout my life the willingness to take risks has helped me move from one opportunity to the next. ***First, I taught myself to recognize opportunities that are in front of me and take advantage of them. Second, if I didn't see any good prospects staring me in the face, I created my own. And finally, I learned to be bold enough to take a chance on my own ideas ... even when the odds were against me.*** It's important to follow this advice: "Imagine you are a turtle. If you go through life too scared to stick your head out of your shell, you're not going to see anything or get anywhere. You've got to stick your neck out."

There were times in my life when I stuck my neck out and it led me many places. There were also times when I stuck my neck out and nearly got my head bitten off. Even then I was glad I had been bold because I knew that *even if taking a chance led to failure, it would teach me something. Failure is only a stepping-stone to success. Taking a chance leads to new directions; it's never a dead end.* Once you understand that, taking a risk seems less "risky." As a very brave and wise New York cab driver recently said to me as he raced wildly through rush-hour traffic: "You can't fail if you never try … and when you try, you never fail!" Everybody's a philosopher! Especially in New York.

Everyone has faced times when taking a new risk seems amazingly scary, especially when the need to find a new direction is not voluntary. Many people want to crawl back into their shells when they lose a job, but not Bloomberg News founder and New York Mayor Michael R. Bloomberg. At age thirty-nine, he was suddenly given the pink slip at work.

"After fifteen years of twelve-hour days and six-day weeks working with the Wall Street bond trading firm of Salomon Brothers—including nine years as a general partner—I was fired," Bloomberg recalls.

Even though he was laid off in style it was still a slap in the face. "I'll be the first to admit that $10 million is a lot more than most people get as their severance pay when they get fired. On the other hand, this was the only full-time job I'd ever had." Now in need of a new one, he looked around and saw no obvious opportunities. "I was in the same boat as an athlete who gets cut from his team after many years of success. Another financial services firm probably didn't want to pick up such a high-priced player."

So what did he do? He created his own opportunity. He stuck his neck out and took a chance. Or, as he says with a chuckle, "I reinvented my professional life—under duress." With his many years of training and experience, he decided to start his own business. He had an idea he believed in and took a gamble. "My idea was based on the belief that access to information, and the ability to act on it, would transform the securities business by leveling the playing field between buyers and sellers," he says. "I set out to develop a user-friendly financial computer system that would not only provide analysis but also form a community or 'network' among securities dealers."

Bloomberg knew he had unique talents and insight that could grow into something bigger if he took the chance.

"Was I prepared to risk an embarrassing and costly failure? Absolutely," says Bloomberg. "Happiness for me has always been the thrill of the unknown. I rented a one-room temporary office with a view of an alley and started a company with four employees and no contracts. Twenty years later, this information network has grown into a multi-billion-dollar business—Bloomberg LP. It's one of the largest financial news, broadcast, and publishing companies in the world."

Mayor Bloomberg is definitely a risk taker at whatever project he puts his mind to. After building his news business into a resounding success, he wholeheartedly jumped into an even bigger venture—running for mayor.

"Now I face my biggest career challenge yet—as New York City's 108th mayor," he says. "New York City is the greatest place in the world. And being its mayor has to be the greatest job in the world."

Create your own opportunity. Find the thrill of the unknown. If something forces you to end one phase of your life, take the time to deal with what has happened and heal from the experience. Find closure through "dealing" and "healing" before you move on. Starting any new venture may seem risky, but be confident that it will lead you to the next interesting adventure in your life.

~

If you don't play, you can't win. I learned that lesson in the political arena. In 1979 John Y. Brown, Jr. and I got married on Saint Patrick's Day in one of the oldest churches in New York, the Marble Collegiate Church, by our mutual spiritual mentor, Dr. Norman Vincent Peale. "Now you two go out into the world," Dr. Peale told us at the end of the ceremony, "and serve God and mankind together."

Well, we took his words to heart. Honeymooning in the Caribbean at Las Samanas, St. Maarten, in a hotel room with a lumpy bed, no carpet, no room service, and low water pressure (I enjoyed the unpretentious simplicity, but John did not), we had a big "serve mankind" question on our minds. John had to decide whether he would run for governor of Kentucky in the upcoming Democratic primary only two months away.

John had grown up around politics—it was part of his life. He had been JFK's campaign chairman in 1960 for the state of Kentucky, and he had always been very involved in Kentucky politics. His father, John Y. Brown, Sr., a statesman and brilliant orator, had been Speaker of the House in Kentucky and a one-time U.S. representative under Franklin D. Roosevelt. He ran for governor many times but never won. John, Jr., had politics in his blood.

In the months leading up to our wedding a close political friend of John's had been telephoning repeatedly, urging him to run for governor. The deadline to decide was in five days, but we were sitting on the fence about it. How could we win a primary with only two months to campaign? All the other candidates had been out there giving "stemwinders on the stump" (rabble-rousing speeches on the courthouse steps) all around the state for years. They had been building momentum.

And then, almost as an omen, we bumped into Jacqueline Onassis. She was vacationing at the same resort, along with her son, John Jr. Standing in the lobby in white cotton pants, white shirt, and sandals, her dark hair pulled back and wearing those signature dark glasses, she was effortlessly glamorous. We said hello and had a brief chat. Underneath Jackie's big, dark shades you could sense a spark. "John," she said to my husband in that famous, breathy voice, "you know … you remind me sooo much of Jack!"

Jack Kennedy, that is. Well. If those aren't encouraging words for a man poised to go into politics, I don't know what words would be. It was truly a magical moment.

Sometimes, when you are about to take a risk, it helps to have a sign. When John and I sat down to lunch, I fixed my eyes on him. "You have to make a decision on this now," I told him. He looked out toward the ocean and was silent. We had been back and forth on this all week. What if we make fools of ourselves? Do we have a chance? Will this be a mistake? What is the right thing to do?

"You've got to stop talking about it," I told him, "and just decide."

"Okay," he agreed, *let's do it*."

We packed up our bags and left St. Maarten the next day. We knew there was work to be done.

Immediately after arriving in Kentucky, we got busy on the phones. I knew that when John had said "Let's do it," we were in this campaign together as partners. John knew I wasn't the kind of wife to stand adoringly behind him; he wanted me by his side.

John called up his trusted advisers, political types, business associates, and high-profile friends. "Listen, I'm thinking about running for governor," he broke the news. "What do you think? Can I have your support?"

"But John, you don't have enough time!" they all insisted. "It just can't be done!"

One after another after another, we got the same reaction. We were stunned. Not one of them said, "Go for it!" Except, I might add, this old-timer we met in a hotel lounge who told us, "If y'all will run, I'll put $5,000 down right now." And he slapped the table really hard. Okay, well, at least *someone* else believed in us.

But the people we knew all told John, "We already have our support with someone else, you can't do it, it will never happen ... you'll never win ... it will never work." And so on.

We called a total of 119 people. Each and every one of them said no. Once again, we had to reassess the situation. Were we making a mistake? It was true that the five other candidates already had all their support lined up.

And what did we have? We had enough belief in ourselves to take the chance. What would it hurt to try? People might laugh at us, sure. But we knew we were a strong team, we had each other, and we were in love. We didn't let everybody's "no's" get to us.

Two days later John announced he was running for governor.

"We'll take the risk and see what happens," he said.

After the announcement we went into overdrive. ***Support your risk taking with hard work. Taking a risk on its own isn't enough. It has to be followed by a great deal of effort. Many people take a leap and don't build the foundation to support it. If you do that, you may fall. But if you take the plunge and work hard to make your idea fly, you increase the likelihood that your risk will be worth it.***

Our campaign had already started on an untraditional note. And let me tell you, it continued that way. First of all, we didn't have a home yet because the house in Lexington we had purchased shortly before our wedding, the historic Cave Hill Place built in 1821, needed major renovations. So we lived in the Hyatt Regency in Louisville, and it became campaign central.

I was tagged the small-talk queen. I loved to go out and talk to everybody, while John was very shy at campaigning. Our political strategist, Bob Squier, called me "flypaper Phyllis" because I'd draw the crowd like bees to honey, and I enjoyed doing it. Then John would appear and give his wonderful speech on his campaign theme, "Kentucky and Company—the state that's run like a business."

John was one of the first businessmen to run for governor, and his campaign platform was to run the state like a thriving industry. And since he was the cofounder and had been chairman of the board of the international fast-food chicken empire, Kentucky Fried Chicken, he had incredible business savvy and experience.

We blitzed the state in a helicopter. We'd land in the middle of a field, in a parking lot, in the hills of Appalachia in rural Kentucky—anywhere we could—and create a dramatic entrance like a big bird dropping out of the sky before greeting the astonished voters.

I wrote a handwritten letter on my stationery that started with the greeting, "Dear Friend," and we sent photocopies to each and every voter. When they saw me in person, they'd say, "Oh, Phyllis, thank you for your letter! I loved hearing from you personally." Everything we did was personalized, innovative, and new for politics, and each step along the way was a risk. And it was a bit unsettling to our opponents.

Even our campaign consultants were wary. During campaign meetings they would propose an agenda and say, "This is how you have to do it." And we'd say, "No, we don't want to do it that way. We want to do it *this* way. We want to try something new."

And of course we would hear, "You can't do that! It's never been done before!"

"*Precisely*," I would say. "That's why we should do it!" My entrepreneurial spirit would kick in. I was learning the truth of the adage that **nothing is carved in stone. If somebody tells you it is, make new carvings.**

I remember walking out of a meeting with the carved-in-stone thinkers completely frustrated. "I don't believe these people!" I said to John. "They just tell us why something *can't* work instead of finding a way to prove it *can*. They suggest these ridiculous ideas and then tell us we should do it." They had a hard time accepting that we knew what was right for us.

We kept on going. As an entrepreneur, John knew we had to follow our own style of doing things, and nine out of ten times, that style wasn't like anybody else's. We started a phone bank of thirty volunteers lined up in one room like political telemarketers. Now it's done all the time, but it was new then. All day they'd call people and talk about John. Every voter in Kentucky must have gotten a call from us at one time or another. We also made some groundbreaking commercials.

For one, John and I got flat on our backs onto a low pulley and were rolled into a coal mine to talk to the miners. It was amazing. We were *everywhere*.

Our opponents and even our consultants were used to playing it safe. But once John took the risk of running for governor, we knew we had to use everything we had. Instinctively, we knew that we were doing the right thing. If you play it safe all the time, which is what most people do, where does that get you? We were fueled by sheer will and the belief that we could do a good job. We were newlyweds with each other to lean on, so we had no fear. In fact, we were still technically on our honeymoon, so the press called our blitz "the honeymoon campaign."

But the honeymoon hadn't begun with the voters yet. As far as we could see, they weren't even at the commitment stage. "He's a nice guy and we really like his wife," we'd hear, "but …"

The first Saturday in May was approaching. We had only two weeks before the primary election. Again we had to ask ourselves: Is it worth it? So far there was no sign that our gamble and hard work were paying off. In other words, we hadn't caught fire. But maybe the people weren't ready yet. Maybe they were hearing us but were not ready to act on it.

At those times you have to keep the faith. "Let's wait until the sun comes out at the Derby," John said, referring to the annual Kentucky Derby always held on the first Saturday in May. "If things don't change this weekend, we'll have to rethink this."

Then the sun came out. I put on my big beautiful hat, and we took the long walk to our fourth-floor table on what they called Millionaires' Row. As we strolled by, we were stopped at least fifty times. "Hey, John! Hey, Miss Phyllis!" "Good luck, John!" "We're rooting for you!"

That Saturday everything changed. Suddenly the enthusiasm started picking up everywhere, and there was a groundswell. We hadn't peaked yet, but we were on our way. Two weeks later we won the primary election in a landslide. We were on a roll. We continued campaigning the same way for the next six months until the general election. Pitted against a former Republican governor, we won. And on that winning night John held his father's hand high into the air, like a prizefighter: "We did it, Dad!"

From the get-go, no one thought we had a chance. Not our friends, our colleagues, the voters, or the press. But we took the risk and were victorious. *Sometimes you just have to take a leap of faith and jump*.

~

When you take the plunge into a new business venture, there is always someone around to tell you not to do it, you can't do it, or you are doing it all wrong. Elaine Kaufman didn't listen, and her risk paid off: Her restaurant grew from a "seedy" building that people thought had no chance into the hippest of New York hangouts. For the last forty years Elaine's restaurant has been the favorite haunt of the New York literary set and the rich and famous. Her regular patrons have included Woody Allen, Tennessee Williams, Al Pacino, Jackie Kennedy Onassis, Frank Sinatra, Marlon Brando, Norman Mailer, Tom Wolfe, Chevy Chase, and Michelle Pfeiffer. A July 2002 *Vanity Fair* story on her success called Elaine's "the Hottest Saloon in the World."

It all started with her dream and the willingness to take the risk to achieve it. In the early 1960s, when very few women got bank loans or opened their own restaurants, Elaine did both. Growing up in Queens and the Bronx, she worked in a used bookstore and a pharmacy before venturing into the restaurant business in 1963. She looked around for a cheap place she could call her own.

"I found this spot on Eighty-eighth Street and Second Avenue," she recalls. The spot was a former Hungarian restaurant in a German neighborhood on the Upper East Side. Yes, it was cheap. But unlike today, at that time the area was not fashionable by a long shot.

"Nobody went to restaurants around there. The area didn't have such a good reputation. It was a working-class neighborhood where people—the nannies, doormen, and housekeepers who worked on Park Avenue—could live cheaply. One of my partners said, 'Oh my God, it's up in Spanish Harlem!' The other one said, 'It's a really, really seedy building, Elaine. Don't do it.' Everyone told me I was making a bad decision. No one said, 'Good luck.'"

When she went to her bank to apply for a loan to buy the restaurant, they also didn't wish her luck. They surely didn't lend her money. "At that time, women just didn't run restaurants," she says. "Women weren't considered good business risks. The banks at that time were not so great at lending money to women, especially if you were not married. But I had my own money—$5,000."

With everything working against her—unpromising location, little money, and a pre-women's liberation mentality— Elaine forged ahead. Pooling her money with her two partners, she bought the place. "Then every piece of furniture I bought came out of the register—tablecloths, chairs, everything. I furnished the restaurant with chairs I found on the Lower East Side for $5 each."

The risk paid off. "No one thought it would work," says Elaine, "but I'm still in business. The people all came, and they still come. I think if you have a dream, you can make it real. You just have to go for it. You have to be prepared to work long hours. Have an open mind. And don't be afraid to find a spot and make it yours."

Elaine saw an opportunity where others didn't, and she took it.

~

Jane Rosenthal, a well-known movie mogul and my dear friend, had the same knack for seeing an opportunity and jumping in when others advised against it. I first met Jane when she was an NYU student majoring in film and television and working part-time with us as a production assistant on *The NFL Today*. Everyone thought she was smart and friendly and had a bright future. A decade later, after producing seventy movies as a television executive at CBS, Jane became a studio executive at Disney, and subsequently at Warner Brothers, in Los Angeles. There her successes continued, and her life looked exciting and challenging, but in truth she was burned out and ready for a change. One day the director Martin Scorsese called her with a new challenge. He urged Jane to leave her job at Warner Brothers, move to New York, and work with Robert De Niro to build a new film company, Tribeca Productions.

It was immediately clear that this was a golden opportunity. "When I was a student at NYU film school, I studied Scorsese's student films," says Jane, "and suddenly here I was talking to the two people who *epitomized* filmmaking and film to me." Now we look at Tribeca's successes and think: How exciting to get involved in something like that when it started! But this was before *Analyze This*, *Analyze That*, *Wag the Dog*, *Meet the Parents*, and *About a Boy*. **That's the hard part about** *taking risks: You have to make the decision before you know how it will turn out!* For Jane the risk was immense.

She was getting no encouragement to make the move. "All of my friends, my advisers, anybody around me I talked to in the industry whom I trusted all said, *'Don't do this.* Don't go work for an actor. Don't move to New York. If you do this, you may as well resign from the industry. You won't be heard from ever again.' It was like I was going to literally fall off the face of the earth. That's how people made it sound to me."

When you face a wall of negativity, taking a chance is all the more challenging. "I really agonized about this decision," Jane says. "Just when I thought I had made up my mind, I'd call Bob up and say, 'You know, why don't you start building without me and I'll come in a year when you have it set up.' 'Why?' De Niro responded. 'Do you want to be a studio executive for the rest of your life?'"

What Jane did next reminds me of what I do when I have to decide whether a risk is worth taking. *Make a list. Write down all the pros and cons. Also, as Jane did, write down the intangibles—the uncertainties that you don't understand well enough to know whether they are pros or cons. Making a list helps you organize your thoughts and identify what's most important to you.* I use big legal pads or sometimes bits of paper, backs of envelopes, whatever I can pick up first when the inspiration hits me and I make a list.

Jane's list helped clarify the situation for her. "I finally went away by myself to think about the whole thing," says Jane. "I sat down and wrote a list of pros, cons, and intangibles. Looking at the list, I realized that the intangibles were basically going to be there for my entire life. There was nothing I could do to change them. And I realized that the pros were all about trusting my own instincts. I came away from that weekend thinking that if I couldn't trust my own instincts, then I didn't belong in this business anyway. This is a business all about instincts and trusting your gut and trusting your beliefs in someone or a piece of material."

Another support for Jane on the pros list was her favorite poem, "If" by Rudyard Kipling. She reread these memorable lines over and over: "If you can trust yourself when all men doubt you, / But make allowance for their doubting too ..." This is one of my favorite poems too, and I've often used it to help me through troubled times.

"I would find myself repeating that poem and saying, okay, maybe they're right, but I know I'm right, too," says Jane. "I knew if I didn't try it, I would always regret it."

She took the risk, packed up, and went to New York. "I rented my house, and I put my car in storage. I left myself some safety net psychologically. My attitude was I'll go do this for a year or two, and if it doesn't work, I'll go back to LA and be a studio executive."

When she arrived in New York, she moved into a tiny apartment that was also the office. "For the first year I was quite miserable. All I did was work. I felt I had a lot to prove to Bob, but I had more to prove to myself. I had to prove that trusting my own instincts had turned into something. At the same time, at the end of the day, I knew it was the right thing for me to do."

The whole experience, Jane says today, "was a huge lesson for me. One of the biggest lessons I ever learned. That I had to take the risk."

Jane has continued to take risks. Most recently, in the summer of 2002, she, her husband, Craig Hatkoff, and Robert De Niro launched a Cannes-style film festival for downtown New York City to help bring new business to lower Manhattan after

9/11. The Tribeca Film Festival was a huge risk, since no one knew if anyone would come, but when 100,000 people attended, the risk paid off.

The bigger the risk, the bigger the payoff. Starting a new company, launching a political campaign, moving across the country for a new job—all are major risks that can seem petrifying. Whether it is your choice or not, you will face such opportunities and must decide whether they are right for you. Remember, you can't possibly know in advance whether it will be "worth the risk." You must base your decision on the information you can gather at the time and how you feel about that information. But don't forget to ask yourself this question as well: If I don't take this risk, will I regret later that I didn't even try?

4

FIND A VOID
AND FILL IT

There's a great line in one of my favorite films, Butch Cassidy and the Sundance Kid, *where Paul Newman (Butch) says to Robert Redford (Sundance): "Kid, I got vision and the rest of the world wears bifocals." That's what it feels like when you're a visionary (all right, Butch was an outlaw, but he was an outlaw with insight). A visionary can see what is out there and, more important, what is not out there. That's how you find a void and fill it.*

Find your niche. It takes someone with a creative spirit and a creative mind to see what is missing. You must then

figure out how to fill in the gaps. It's entrepreneurs who can see what others can't. When you zero in on your own unique talent or idea and it's something no one else is doing, you've found your niche.

As someone who has had a rather eclectic career, I've been lucky enough to find my niche more than once. In the 1970s, I was on the cover of *People* magazine as the "First Lady of the Locker Room." In the 1980s, I was again on the cover of *People* as the "First Lady of Kentucky." In the 1990s, my best one yet: *Poultry Processing* magazine put me on their cover as the "First Lady of Chicken." Now I can die a happy woman!

In 1986, I founded a company called Chicken by George that started a revolution in the retail chicken business. Remember, it wasn't so long ago when you couldn't buy prepared chicken breasts in the local grocery store. Chicken was sold either whole or in pieces. The only way you could buy skinned and boned chicken breasts was if the butcher did it for you, and if you wanted it marinated, you had to do it yourself. I started a company in my kitchen to sell boneless, skinless, marinated chicken breasts. This new product met with resistance from grocers at first, but it caught on immediately with consumers. We grew the company locally and, later, nationally after it became a division of Hormel (you'll read more about this later in the chapter).

Chicken by George filled a void in the marketplace and ultimately led all the major chicken companies to launch their own versions. Although the product is taken for granted today, people didn't know they needed it until we introduced it. My chicken idea emerged from my busy lifestyle as a working mother. I could instantly see the potential for a product that would save time and energy. *Imagine yourself as a consumer of your own life. What would make your life easier? What do you find frustrating, difficult, or too time-consuming? What new product or service might help? If you have an idea that would help you, it might help others as well. Thinking like this is key to being an entrepreneur.*

Like my idea with Chicken by George, my friend Richard Kirshenbaum's innovations sprang from his own experience. Today, Kirshenbaum, Bond, & Partners is one of the largest advertising agencies in the United States, with over half a billion dollars in billings. Richard started it with an idea that was new in the advertising world.

I first learned about Richard when I read an article about his small, new advertising agency, Kirshenbaum and Bond, in *New York* magazine sixteen years ago. He and his business partner were nicknamed "the Ad Brats" because they were young and dared to do things differently. Sounded good to me. After reading the article, I immediately called him, set up a meeting in New York, spent twenty minutes with them, and hired the firm to do promotion for Chicken by George. Since we were both startup companies, we were a good match for each other.

Earlier in his career, Richard had been dissatisfied with what he saw as a young copywriter at J. Walter Thompson, a big New York advertising firm. "I felt there needed to be a new voice in the advertising arena," he says. "Consumers had grown up in the 1960s with TV commercials and sitcoms where everything was happy-happy, nothing ever went wrong, and everything was always wrapped up in thirty seconds or thirty minutes with a smiling point of view. And while I'm not a negative person, I thought there needed to be a more realistic and sophisticated voice."

He envisioned an ironic kind of advertising that played to audiences with wit. He saw a void and knew how to fill it. When he tried to convince his boss to let him try some bold

new ideas, he was told no. But Richard and his business partner, Jon Bond, had a feeling about this new direction and were
determined to see their ideas on the glossy pages of major
magazines in the future. They teamed up and began approaching clients on a freelance basis.

One of Richard's first calls was to the office of Kenneth
Cole, the famous shoe designer. He was told Cole had no time
for a meeting, but that didn't stop him. "I made friends with
his secretary, which is one of the key things I've learned in life:
Make friends with the secretaries and the assistants! I'd
call her every day, and we started having this funny, ongoing
dialogue." With charm and humor, he got an appointment.
The meeting lasted a nanosecond.

"Kenneth said: 'I hate advertising. Nice to meet you, but
I'm just not interested.'"

Richard wasn't giving up. "Before I leave your office, Mr.
Cole, I want to ask you one question. Do you think your ads
are great?"

Cole hesitated. "No, I don't. What do *you* think about them?"

"I don't think they're great either," Richard said.

"Well, if you ever come up with something 'great,' you can
show it to me," said Cole, ushering Richard out of the office.

Hello, opportunity. A foot was in the door. Now all Richard
had to do was use his talent to develop something innovative
that would be exciting to Cole. Richard and Jon spent all night
designing a new idea: "It was very simple: a blank page that
quoted Cole as saying, 'Imelda Marcos bought 2,700 pairs of
shoes … she could have at least had the courtesy to buy one of
ours!' You didn't even see the product."

In an era of straightforward informational ads, this was a
breakthrough. "First of all, no one had ever done an ad where
you didn't see the product," says Richard. "Second, it was

using what I called a 'negative' sell. He didn't say she *bought* a pair of his shoes; he actually said she *didn't* buy a pair. I went to Kenneth the next day and showed it to him. He took one look, loved it, and said: *'Print it!'*"

The ad was a hit and started a whole new trend in the advertising business. Even Richard's very unvisionary boss wanted to get on the bandwagon. "After the ad came out, he came into my office, slammed the ad down on the table, and said, 'Why can't we do ads like this?'" Richard says. "'I did that ad,' I told him, 'and I quit!'"

The next day, Richard and Jon started their own agency, against the advice of colleagues and prospective clients. But they knew better—and so did Kenneth Cole, who encouraged them. "It's all about the ideas," Cole told them. And their ideas were fresh and exciting and created a punch in the stale advertising arena. Today they use their offbeat creativity to "reinvent" the images of big-name products like Snapple, Coach, and Meow Mix.

Dare to be different. What propelled Richard from an unknown copywriter to one of the most successful advertising executives in America were his original ideas, his gut instinct, and his vision. In business, you are constantly guessing about the ever-changing needs of consumers. If you can predict and satisfy those needs, you are finding a void and filling it.

But be forewarned. When you venture into uncharted territory, you can expect resistance from the people around you. A pioneer must develop a thick skin; what you see as a void usually looks like trouble to those who want to maintain the status quo.

My amazing friend Ann Richards is known today as the popular, feisty, and smart former governor of Texas who has been a strong voice for the Democratic party and for women in politics. Over the course of her career Ann has used her intelligence, integrity, courage, and humor—combined with her incredible presence—to become one of the most success-ful women in America. She is a wonderful role model, and I'm thrilled that she is now spending most of her time in New York as one of the partners in Public Strategies Inc.

But on her way to success she encountered many obsta-cles. When she decided to run for her first political position—county commissioner of Travis County—people told her that position would be too difficult to fill. The county commission-er was in charge of the rural roads and water problems as well as running the courthouse system.

"Very few women had ever been county commissioner in the entire state," says Ann. "If they were, it was because their husbands had died and they had then run for the unexpired term and got elected in their stead. When it came time for them to run in their own right and get reelected, most of them didn't do it or were unsuccessful."

Ann wasn't daunted by the prospect of being the first. Growing up in the 1950s, she'd been told all her life that there were things she couldn't do because "only boys could do that." She hadn't gotten much encouragement in school either. The only women in her textbooks were nurses—Clara Barton and Florence Nightingale—and occasionally Eleanor Roosevelt, but only because she was the wife of a president. "Textbooks never gave girls the idea that they might aspire to do anything other than be a homemaker, work in healthcare, or teach school," Ann remembers.

Fortunately, this budding pioneer had a secret weapon. "My father always told me I could do anything I wanted to, be anything I wanted to be," she says. "He encouraged me to reach for the stars. I can remember him holding me up to a mirror and saying, 'You see that girl? That's the smartest little girl in the world!'"

But when Ann made an untraditional career move, most folks weren't ready for something new just yet. "I was going around trying to talk to the leadership and the business community about my aspirations. And I went to see one man and said, 'I'm Ann Richards and I'm seeking the office of county commissioner.' And he looked at me with this very puzzled look. And he said, 'You think you're gonna grade the roads?'

"And I said, 'Well, no, sir, I don't think I personally will grade the roads. But then, I don't know very many businessmen who type their own letters. I think I can find someone who can operate the machinery.'"

The man didn't stop there. "But ... why would you want to do something like this?" he next asked. "Did you hate your daddy or something?"

Ann laughs about it today when she tells this story to women's groups and in business lectures. She had the last laugh, of course, because she did go on to defeat her opponent, who had held the position for twelve years. And that first successful election launched her into a respected career in politics.

If no one has done it, be the first. When there are no role models for you to emulate, create your own role and fill it. Think of yourself as a pioneer leading the way into undiscovered territories. All it takes is one person to go ahead and soon the others will follow.

∾

Ann Richards and Richard Kirshenbaum both sensed that a change was imminent in their professions before the people around them perceived it. I felt the same way when I started my chicken business.

It was 1986. I had just left my job at the *CBS Morning News* and the hubbub of New York City to live in Kentucky full-time and be with my two children and my husband, John, who was contemplating a run for the Senate. I was loving every leisurely minute of my time at home. Away from big-city demands and deadlines for the first time in fifteen years, I spent my days taking the kids to soccer and T-ball games, school plays, and dance and piano lessons. I was perfectly content to be just "Mom."

Then one day John called me into a meeting he was having in the breakfast room. Dennis Hook, a businessman and family friend, was presenting his ideas for a new business venture: selling a variety of prepared chicken products to restaurants. His samples included boneless, skinless chicken breasts marinated in several flavors.

"Try some, Phyllis," he urged me, pointing to the teriyaki-marinated chicken breast on a plate. I tasted it. "Mmm, this is good," I said. "And it's good for you. This would be great to have at home." I had visions of my mother cutting up chicken parts at the kitchen counter for our evening meal. I hated that messy preparation, and who had time to do all that work?

Dennis asked me why I didn't figure out a way to do it.

"Do it?" I replied. "Me? Do *what*?"

"Start a company to make marinated chicken breasts available at home! You can call it 'Chicken, by George.'"

"What, are you out of your mind?" I answered. "Put my name on *chicken*? Perfume, jewelry, clothing—maybe. But not chicken!"

Later that day, however, I was still thinking about this insane idea. I wrote the name "Chicken by George" on the back of an envelope and decided it was clever. I liked it. It had a ring to it. But me go into business? An entrepreneur? Well, I *had* always thought I was an entrepreneur at heart, so that part made sense to me. And I wanted to have time for my children while keeping active professionally, but on my own terms and my own timetable. I thought about the market for such a product. If I was a working mom who rushed home after a hard day at work to prepare a family dinner, what a relief it would be to whip up a quick, healthy meal that was low-fat, low-cal, and tasty. It would be such a time-saver to have delicious gourmet chicken in different flavors at my fingertips. There was nothing out there like this ... but there should be.

Lightning struck! There was nothing out there like this. But there should be. Here was a void that needed filling! Okay, so I didn't know anything about starting a chicken business. But I was a mother, and I knew what my family needed.

I called up my friend Harriet Dupree, who was an excellent chef, and we got to work in my kitchen. We mixed up different flavorings—lemon herb, country mustard dill, tomato herb with basil, Cajun, teriyaki, mesquite barbecue, Italian bleu cheese—and we put chicken breasts into baggies to marinate overnight. The next day I invited a group of friends to dinner; unknown to them, they were my focus group. Over the coming months, this was how we did our "product research and development" until we had perfected the recipes and the concept. Our eventual packaging would contain a marinated four-ounce lean chicken breast, ready to cook in minutes by baking, broiling, sautéing, microwaving, grilling—whatever your fancy.

I had officially become a "mompreneur"! That's an entrepreneur who starts a new business that enables her to be with her family and work at the same time.

After a year, we had outgrown my kitchen. We opened a small two-room office and test kitchen in Louisville and hired one employee, Kerry Kramp (now CEO of his own company, Buffets Inc.). Kerry's expertise in product development and John's guidance and support were crucial to our eventual success. ***Having knowledgeable people around you helps to minimize the inevitable problems of any startup company.*** Now that we had our product, the next step was to get it into grocery stores, but I had no credibility as a businesswoman or chef. Who was going to listen to me? I went to several of the grocery store chains in Kentucky and tried to convince the general managers and their meat buyers to sell my chicken. As you can already imagine, I was told it would never work. (Ahh—that word "never" was becoming music to my ears. To me it meant a "challenge"!)

"Phyllis, it's certainly new and different," they would say, "but people will never buy it. It's *too* new and different." I saw that talking was not enough. They had to taste it. So on each stop, we prepared the chicken for them and gave them a taste. "It's delicious, but people aren't going to buy marinated, ready-to-cook chicken!" they insisted. "They aren't ready for it."

I couldn't have disagreed more! I believed that being new and different was what would make it a success. I knew that it would fill a void and that people would love it once they tried it.

I finally convinced one manager in a Kroger store in Louisville to give it a chance. On test day, they set up a small electric skillet and began cooking samples and passing them out to customers. I sneaked into the store incognito wearing a baseball cap, sunglasses, and sweats to watch. I didn't want anyone at that point to know that I was the "George" in Chicken by George. I wanted the product to work on its own. I knew people would like it, but they had to be educated to this new concept. I also didn't want any critics to say, "What is Phyllis up to now?" Hiding behind an end-aisle display around the produce department, I could hear the customers' reactions. "This is great!" they were saying. "It's so different. I love it! This will make my life so easy." It was like we were the Baskin-Robbins of chicken. Many marinades to choose from. Pick a flavor, any flavor. Customers were buying six chicken breasts in different marinades at a time.

Later we packaged the chicken in a crisp, clean white box with a see-through window and my picture, a red and blue logo, and "By George" in my handwriting in white on a slash of red. In the beginning I was uncomfortable seeing my face on a chicken box, but when you're a startup company sometimes you don't have money to advertise. So we had to use any competitive advantage we had to catch consumers' attention, and my name and face were known. We were also the first to put nutritional information on a package of meat (now, of course, it's a requirement). The chicken had no MSG and was low-fat and low-calorie. Customers loved it.

Soon we were in stores across the state, and we were getting 80 percent repeat business. The product was taking off and creating a buzz in the local chicken industry. Remember, this is Kentucky—home of Kentucky Fried Chicken—and people there take their chicken seriously! Maybe my chicken didn't have eleven herbs and spices, but we had eight marinades and a special marinating process that we developed for the chicken.

When you take an idea into the marketplace, you must learn its distinctive language, so soon I became a chicken expert. I roamed the aisles of supermarkets and inspected store shelves. I learned about SKUs, product specifications, and grocery store shelf life, the same way I had learned football stats earlier in my career. Who would have thought it? I would walk into stores, see my name and face on the chicken box, and swell with pride.

Sometimes if the boxes weren't all lined up neatly, the meat manager would catch me straightening them and rush over to help. Talking with the manager also gave me a chance to sell a little and ask if it was possible for us to get a few more "facings" (displaying the product "face out") to make a bigger display. We were one of the first companies to get display space in the poultry section right alongside the "boring" chicken parts.

At this time the only other woman doing this kind of homemade entrepreneurial venturing was Debbie Fields with her cookies. She was the Cookie Lady; now I was becoming the Chicken Lady.

We realized we had a hit on our hands as we went from one store to 124 in two years. The *Wall Street Journal* ran an article on me on the front page of the business section that posed this question and answer: "After you've been a beauty queen and a newscaster ... what's next? ... Chicken by George." With a business growing so fast in the local market, I soon realized we needed the arms and legs of a big company to distribute the product on a national level. We went to the major grocery stores, but no one would bite. Once again I heard, "This will never work. Individual chicken breasts in a box? This is too different for the consumers of America." It was also too different for the meat buyers because the chicken was sold fresh and our packages required new handling procedures. The concept had never been tried before.

Lesson: Keep moving forward. If you believe in your idea, don't be satisfied with initial success. Keep the momentum going. Take it to the next level.

The national chains' reactions were discouraging, but we didn't give up. The following week, the Food of the Future show was in Cincinnati, and once again Dennis urged me on. "Why don't you take Chicken by George to the show?" he asked. This time, John was hesitant. "No way," he said to us. "These are the big boys! Phyllis can't play with them; they are in a whole other league. Don't go. You'll embarrass yourself. Besides, who's going to pay the hefty entry fee?" I said, "I am." Having learned my lesson about naysayers years earlier, I used John's doubts to motivate me, paid the fee myself, and began to prepare something new to catch attention at the show.

At times like this, let your imagination run wild! When you're small, you have to be creative to get your point across. If you're a startup company in a competitive market, you need something catchy to get people's attention. We knew our product was good, but we had to get people to try it. The advantage is that when it's your own company, you can try creative tactics the established giants would find way too daring. I did several things. I dressed up my friend Chase in a kooky yellow seven-foot-tall chicken costume to wander the show and direct people to our display. And I put a team of wholesome young women in white Chicken by George baseball hats and sweatshirts and called them the "Phyllettes." They served samples of the chicken to the buyers who stopped by our booth. Can you picture it? A giant chicken, some charming women, potential customers nibbling on our chicken, and me, the founder, beaming over the scene like a proud mother hen.

There I was, a small startup company rubbing shoulders with Kraft, General Foods, and even Tyson's, one of the biggest chicken companies in the world along with Perdue. I was feeling *pretty* pleased with myself until … I glanced over at the Tyson's display and what did I see? Some might call it the ultimate in flattery, but it didn't feel that way to me. They had copied my idea! We had heard the rumor that Tyson's had come to Louisville to scout out our product after the *Wall Street Journal* story ran. Now, they had their own version of boneless, marinated, skinless chicken breasts. My product was health-conscious, and it was sold in a clean white box as if it had been freshly prepared by the butcher. Theirs was in a yellow box, had additives, and was not nearly as low in fat or calories. Of course, competition is what business is all about and I couldn't blame them for trying, but there was no comparison in the quality of the products. Still, the competition would cut into my market share. Plus, when I swallowed my anxiety and went over to compliment Don Tyson on his new product line, he told me they were going to launch the product with $15 million in advertising its first year. And here I was worried about paying the entry fee to the show!

My spirit was zapped, my enthusiasm deflated. How could my small company compete with this national billion-dollar brand? My initial thought was to pack up my chicken samples, gather the Phyllettes and Chase the Chicken, and go home to roost. But I'm not a quitter by nature, so I forced myself to stick it out until the end of the day. As I was leaving, I thought to myself that maybe John was right. Maybe I was dreaming too big. Maybe ...

Just then, I bumped into Dick Knowlton, the chairman of the George A. Hormel Company, a $3.5 billion company famous for putting ham and other pork products (including SPAM) on the dinner tables of America and the world.

"Hey, Phyllis! Love your chicken!" he said, in earnest. "Remember me? Dick Knowlton." He reminded me that we'd danced together fourteen years ago when I emceed the Miss Minnesota pageant.

Did I remember this man? Vaguely. Fourteen years was a long time. Still, I smelled opportunity. "Oh suuuure, I remember dancing with you, Mr. Knowlton!" I replied, with a bright smile. "How are you?!"

We talked a few minutes, and then came the clincher. "We're looking to get into the chicken business," he said. "Is your company for sale?"

"Why, sure, Mr. Knowlton," I beamed. "Anything's for sale at the right price!"

"Give me a call and let's talk," he responded, handing me a business card.

After he left, I rushed to the nearest pay phone and called John. "Guess what?" I said excitedly. "You advised me not to come here ... but I was just talking to the chairman of Hormel and he's interested in buying Chicken by George!"

The moral of the story? Dance with anyone who asks you because they may buy your company some day!

After that meeting we entered into negotiations with Hormel, traveling back and forth to the company's home office in Austin, Minnesota. After several months we became a division of the George A. Hormel Company, and Hormel's Chicken by George was soon to be available across the country. But it turns out that there was nothing *automatic* about taking Chicken by George national; now we had to take the same process I had followed in Kentucky and repeat it in every grocery store chain across the country. Part of our agreement was that I would be the spokesperson for the brand and travel around the country promoting the product. For five years I did national commercials and promotional tours that included personal appearances and interviews on radio, on television, and in newspapers in every major market. On those trips I also met with more grocery store managers and meat buyers than I could keep track of. And once again, in nearly every conversation, I met with resistance. This is when I really learned what is required when you want to introduce something new.

Having a good product is only the beginning; follow-through is essential. The education process is as important as anything. When it's new, people don't know they need it; you must explain why they do. Making a success of something new requires hard work, perseverance, tenacity, enthusiasm, energy, and passion—plus an unwavering belief that you have something that is so special that the consumer can't do without it.

I never dreamed it would be so hard. But it was a dream come true for our small company, and it worked: Chicken by George still has a major following across the country. After sixteen years it is still in many cities and major chains (fresh produce laws and shelf space limitations have kept it out of New York City, so many of my friends have never been able to buy it).

In spite of the hard work required, Ann, Richard, and I will all tell you that our ventures have been worth it. Finding voids and filling them are part of the entrepreneurial spirit that keeps America great. Join us! *Find something you are passionate about that will fill a void. Use all your creativity and imagination and let your idea evolve. Then try every avenue you can to get your idea out there. Give people what they want before they even know they want it. And remember that follow-through on everything is key. Now, go for it!*

5

TRUST YOUR INSTINCTS

My first big assignment after joining the CBS Sports team was to interview the star quarterback for the New York Jets, Joe Namath. I had successfully completed a thirteen-week option period, and the network executives had given me a three-year contract. Still, some were dubious as to whether I could do it, and some wanted me to fail. Here was my chance to prove to those who believed in me that their support was justified.

Everyone has first-day job jitters, but I was especially nervous because the test of my ability would appear on national television. If I messed up, many eyes would be watching! Plus, Namath was the premier sports celebrity of the day. Other star athletes were big; Namath was bigger than big. To make matters worse, I had met him years earlier when he was guest hosting the *Tonight Show* and I was one of the guests. Our interaction had been brief that evening, but I wasn't sure we'd hit it off.

On this occasion we got off to a bad start. I was to interview him just before practice at the Jets' training camp outside of New York City. After the crew set up the cameras, we waited for him. And waited. And waited. He finally arrived over an hour late and in a testy mood. The clock was ticking, and he was nervous about getting to practice on time because pro ball players were fined if they were late.

When Joe and I finally sat down together, I started with some formalities to ease into the interview. Then I had to decide: Do I ask him the tough question now? Or do I save it for the end? It was my journalistic style—as well as that of many of my colleagues—to ask the more challenging questions toward the end of the interview, so if the interviewee got upset and took off, you already had material in the can.

My instincts this time, however, told me to ignore my usual approach and go for it. I had this feeling I had to get Namath to say something revealing—and *fast*. So a minute or so into the interview I decided to ask the question everyone wanted him to answer.

The Jets hadn't been doing well that season, and Namath had yet to address their losing streak in any interviews. And who would *want* to ask about it? Namath had an intimidating presence and a history of winning; his leadership had been instrumental in the Jets' victory at the Super Bowl five years earlier. Indeed, my feature producer, Louis Schmidt, told me later that the more seasoned male reporters would have never asked him that question. After all, he was Joe Namath! Still, I felt intuitively that I had to seize the moment.

"You know, Joe," I asked, "the Jets look pretty bad this year. Do you take responsibility for that?" I had no idea what response I'd get.

Namath bristled at first. Then he kind of chuckled. He said he couldn't say the team wasn't bad. After all, though it was early in the season, their record was one and four. Then he admitted he had to take full responsibility for the situation. He started talking about the team's morale and his feelings about the losing streak until we were interrupted a minute or so later by the earsplitting roar of a lawn mower outside the window. We stopped taping, and Lou rushed out to ask the guy to turn the darn thing off for a few minutes until we finished. I struggled to conceal my frustration: Namath was beginning to open up, and I didn't want to lose the moment.

But when Lou returned, he found me standing up, almost in tears. Joe was also on his feet, unhooking the microphone from his shirt and saying he had to go because he was late. Then he bolted from the room.

Lou and I stood there, dumbfounded. We had less than three minutes on tape! Nevertheless, when we went back to the editing room and reviewed the interview, we realized we had an amazing sound bite. In those mere 180 seconds Namath had revealed more about himself than he had elsewhere all season. I had zeroed in on the right question, and it had worked.

When the interview aired the following Sunday on *The NFL Today*, fans and media alike were impressed with the superstar's honesty and my ability to get him to open up. So was the CBS Sports hierarchy.

I had trusted my instincts in that moment, and it had worked. It was a lesson I'd been learning for many years. When I was growing up, my parents would tell me, "When you're not sure what to do, Phyllis, trust your instincts." I wanted to take their advice, but I wasn't always sure what they meant. Instinct wasn't something I could see or touch, so how would I know what it was?

Now I can describe the feeling, a few rounds of life experience later. *It's when you feel something so strongly in the pit of your stomach that you can't ignore it. It's when an idea comes to you, and maybe you don't even know where it came from, but it feels amazingly right. It's when a voice speaks inside you that confirms you are on to something. It says this is right for you; do this no matter what others may say.* Often the noise around us makes it impossible to hear that inner voice, so you need to find a quiet place to push aside the distractions and listen. For me that may be during a walk in the park or a drive in the car by myself or at home alone. That's the only way I can *hear* what my true feelings are.

After you've become attuned to your instincts, the next step is learning to trust them. It comes down to this: *If it feels right, do it. If it feels wrong, don't.* I have found the more I've paid attention to my inner feelings, the more I've moved in the right direction.

Sounds simple, right? Well, it's simple to say but not so simple to do. Everyone has instincts, and listening to your inner voice is always a good idea. But when you're making a decision, whether it's asking one question in an interview or making a major career move, listening to your instincts is necessary but not sufficient. You need it, but it's not all you need.

Learning how to use your instincts as a guide in decision making requires effort. After all, no one's instincts are always correct; so how do you know when to follow them and when to ignore them? Following your intuition could cause you to make impulsive decisions that you regret in an instant (you'll read about one of mine in Chapter 9). *The key is to learn how to use your instincts to support, not dictate, your decisions.*

Use your experience to assess the situation. Your past experience gives you the basis for judging whether your instincts can be trusted.

Had I walked directly into the Namath interview from the runway of the Miss America pageant, I probably would have asked the wrong questions. But at the time of the interview, I had interviewed professional athletes before, so I had experience to tell me what to expect. I had been working in television since I'd been Miss America, and I'd been a sports fan all my life. That week I had done my homework on Namath and the Jets, so I knew what I wanted to ask him. I also knew which questions might be more difficult for him to answer.

My decision to ask the hard questions early was not a whim; it was based on a feeling that grew out of my experience.

On the somewhat loftier plane of hard political news, legendary CBS News anchorman Walter Cronkite told me recently about a time when he followed his instincts to propose a new format in the coverage of presidential politics. No one in the history of television news is more respected than my friend Walter. For decades he ended the *CBS Evening News* with his distinctive "And that's the way it is"—and Americans believed him. He was not only the voice of the news; he was the voice of authority. But in the 1960 political campaign he wanted to try something new.

In that campaign, Cronkite says, "I wanted to do a separate, hourlong interview with Senator Kennedy and Vice President Nixon for one of our broadcasts. We had been debating what kind of program we would do during that period of time, and I suggested something new and different. I wanted to do a program that would be totally unrehearsed and one in which the candidates wouldn't know the questions in advance. I would walk in one door and they would walk in another. We'd sit down, and I'd start throwing tough questions at them."

"Now this kind of format is not so new to anybody today," he explains, "but in 1960 you didn't do things this way in television. So I was told, 'You'll never get the people to do it!' I was told this by the CBS News management and also by Westinghouse, our sponsor for the series of programs we did between the political conventions and the elections that year. They all told me that I would never get the candidates, that they would never agree to do it."

But Walter had a strong feeling he was on to something and refused to be discouraged. He kept making telephone calls and seeking support from every angle he could think of. "I talked to their friends," he says, "I worked on their advisers— explaining the idea to them until they saw my point of view and would present it to the candidates. The thing I try to tell young reporters is that what is required in our business as journalists is persistence. *If you have an idea you believe to be worthy, you should not shy from using every possible means to achieve that goal—assuming the goal we're talking about is legitimate, legal, fair, and honest.*"

All that effort eventually paid off when the candidates agreed to do the interview the way he wanted. As a result, television history was made. Walter had used his experience as a veteran newsman to take his idea and make it a success.

Trusting his instincts developed as a journalist gave Walter Cronkite the fortitude to fight for his idea and to convince those who initially resisted it. That experience illustrates another important aspect of learning to trust your instincts: *If you are relying on your instincts, you should be able to explain to others why following them is a good idea. If something feels right to you and you are passionate about it, that's a great start, but it is essential for you to be able to communicate that passion to those who will help you put your idea into action.* If you can't articulate why it feels right to you, that may be a clue that it isn't.

One of the brightest stars among the new women political leaders for the twenty-first century is Senator Mary Landrieu, who was elected to the U.S. Senate from Louisiana in 1996. Mary is making important contributions in several areas of public policy. She is the first Democratic woman named to the Armed Services Committe, and also serves on committees on energy and natural resources, small business, and appropriations.

I'm a big fan of Mary's. I've been impressed with her warmth, her intelligence, and her ability to have a family and still be a busy public servant. But I was interested to learn that one of the turning points in her rise to national politics grew out of once following her instincts. Mary had been in the state legislature for eight years, representing a district in inner-city New Orleans. In that job she had become known as a champion of issues like women's and children's rights, race relations, and civil rights. Some of her efforts put her at odds with the more conservative majority members of the legislature. "Of course," she says, "in a legislature that was predominantly male, older, more rural, and maybe less progressive, talking about rights for victims of domestic violence and funding for programs for abused children were not necessarily the most popular issues. But I persisted and was pretty effective in that."

Yet she wanted to do more. "I was ready to do something else," Mary says, "so I decided I'd run for state treasurer. Very few people, if any, thought this was a good idea. Even friends kept saying, 'You don't look like a treasurer, you don't act like a treasurer, you haven't championed issues a treasurer would—hard finance and accounting.' I was on the appropriations committee, and I definitely understood the state budget, but I just had a different sense of the office."

It was a sense of the office no one seemed to understand. "It wasn't that people didn't believe in me or thought I shouldn't run for statewide office," she says. "It was that they weren't convinced I had the right profile to run for that particular office. People would say, 'Why don't you run for insurance commissioner?'" she recalls. "'You could be a great consumer advocate. Or why don't you run for lieutenant governor?'"

But she wanted to be the treasurer. "I knew I could take that office and change it. I wanted to help our state get a handle on the financial situation and become better at managing money. Not only could this role help bring better fiscal management and greater accountability to state government, it also could help with building projects to make the state more prosperous in the future."

In the end Mary ran for the office, and in spite of having the least money of all the candidates as well as limited name recognition in the northern part of the state, she won. "I just had my mind made up that this was what I wanted to do," she says today. "It was the right thing for me. It was the way I wanted to serve the state."

She learned to trust her instincts as well. "It was the first time I made a major decision when the crowd wasn't one hundred percent with me." Mary may not have had the crowd with her, but she had drawn on her experience as a seasoned politician and could clearly explain why she was so convinced *her* instincts were right and others were wrong.

~

Like journalists and politicians, business entrepreneurs often need to use their instincts to navigate new opportunities. I had firsthand experience with this when I was one of a group that took the small cottage industry of Kentucky crafts and transformed it into an international business, building on a passion that I had.

When I first moved to Kentucky as a newlywed in the spring of 1979, I felt an immediate emotional attachment to that beautiful state. It didn't take me long to connect with the craftspeople who worked away in the hills and hollows of the land, quietly creating beautiful works of art. I discovered their work during John's campaign for governor. Many times we would swoop down into a small town in our helicopter, I would go off on my own and explore the area while John made his political speeches and shook hands.

Of course, my explorations always led me to the local stores for shopping. On those expeditions I'd find the most beautiful handmade quilts, woven baskets, hand-carved figures, and one-of-a-kind pottery, all made by local craftspeople. We traveled from eastern Kentucky to the lake regions of the west, from the largest cities and suburbs of Louisville and Lexington to the smallest farms in the bluegrass country. In every town, in every crevice, I'd find unique treasures that astounded me, and I'd load up the helicopter with my finds.

"Phyllis, what are you going to do with all this stuff?" people would ask me. No one understood why I was making such a fuss. But sometimes it takes an outsider with a fresh eye to come in and appreciate what is there. Soon my discoveries became more than a hobby; they became a passion—and one I wanted to share with my friends and the rest of the world. In that period I was rushing around New York and Kentucky, busy all the time, and what I valued most about these works was the *time* the artists put into each work. Each object is the result of one individual's creative vision and hours of painstaking work with his or her own hands. I discovered then—and still feel today—that looking at one of these works calms me and helps me slow down.

But it was more than the objects that appealed to me; it was the people. These artisans had a purity and honesty about them that I had rarely found in the other businesses I had worked in. They seemed to possess the same pioneer spirit that had driven many of their ancestors across the mountains to create new lives for themselves in Kentucky. I had a strong feeling for these people and their work. I realized that the creative work of the hand was becoming a lost art and that the craftspeople were becoming a vanishing breed. I was motivated to do something to keep it alive.

At the time I was discovering this new passion, I was still commuting back and forth from Kentucky to New York in my work as a sportscaster. While I was in New York, a favorite pastime was walking down Madison Avenue window-shopping and browsing through the boutiques. One day I stopped in at The Gazebo, a shop known for its handmade items, and was surprised to find that most of their quilts, baskets, and bowls were made in Hong Kong, The Philippines, Japan, Haiti, China, and Tahiti. And most of them were not nearly as interesting as the things I had seen in my travels around Kentucky. At that time, very few were made in America. As one of my campaign promises as first lady, I wanted to promote the arts and crafts of the state in the rest of the country.

A daunting task indeed. We were moving into the glitz and glamour, "greed is good" 1980s. And I intended to bring quilts into the equation?

"Go ahead and try, Phyl," people told me, "but this is not what America wants right now. This is not the style. No one wants homemade *anything*."

But I had the advantage of having one foot in Kentucky and one in New York, so I had experience from both worlds to draw on. My instincts told me something would be needed to balance the glitz and glamour. To everything there is a season, and I knew the country would inevitably want simple, down-to-earth comforts again. I was living in the heartland, and I could feel it in my bones. And these artists were the ones who could provide it. Family roots and traditions were the origin of their craft since many of them learned their art from their parents and grandparents, passed down from generation to generation. If the 1980s heralded a trend of superslick glamour, then the way I saw it, crafts could be the *anti*-trend.

I was increasingly convinced these products had broader commercial potential. My commitment to craft had been born of an instinct, but now I was finding the specific rationale needed to support what I wanted to do with it.

After John was elected governor, I cofounded the non-profit Kentucky Art and Craft Foundation and Gallery, and with Arts Commissioner Lois Mateus, I established a Kentucky Craft Marketing promotion program. Our second step was to sponsor craft markets for the hundreds of local craftspeople to showcase their handmade items. As word spread, gift and specialty buyers came from around the country to see these wares for the first time. To create a buzz, I sent handmade items to friends living in different parts of the country: woven shawls, quilts, baby blankets, hand-carved ducks, and baskets. Each time I sent off another gift to a friend, I felt that I was giving away future heirlooms, pieces of art that could be treasured and passed down through generations. And each time, the friend would ask, "Where did you find this? Where can I get more?"

~

When you have a gut feeling that something will work, tell someone else about it and see what they say. It will help you refine your initial idea and make it stronger. Plus, you will begin to gain allies in support of your idea. I spent many hours explaining to people what was so special about these objects. It was often a hard sell. I had to overcome their initial skepticism and help them see things in a new way. But when I began receiving a positive response, I started to see how far we could go with what was an initial hunch for me.

Then came the turning point. I attended the Democratic National Convention in New York, and the then-chairman of Bloomingdale's, Marvin Traub, hosted a party in his store for all the governors' wives. Here was my chance. At the time Bloomingdale's was showcasing a collection of art objects from China. Marvin would point proudly to a unique piece in the China collection, and I would find myself saying, "But Marvin, you have to see the beautiful Bybee pottery being hand-fired by four generations of one family in a barn in Waco, a small town in Kentucky" or "That Chinese tapestry is lovely, but I've discovered extraordinary hand-sewn quilts in Kentucky that make beautiful wall hangings, and they're *made right here in America.*"

Here I was taking advantage of another lesson I'd learned in following one's instincts: *Trust your instincts for the right moment to ask for support for your idea. Prepare your best arguments and keep them in your pocket at all times, because you must be ready to seize the moment when it comes. When someone says, "Tell me about it," don't hesitate a moment; plunge right into your key points.*

Marvin Traub laughed and told me I was the best sales-person he'd ever seen. He agreed the timing was right for Kentucky craft and asked me to send him some samples.

Within a few days he had a box of bowls, quilts, and Shaker boxes on his desk. Marvin and the buyers at Bloomingdale's loved what they saw and immediately dispatched scouts to cross Kentucky to find craft and folk art. The "Oh! Kentucky" boutique opened at Bloomingdale's to the music of Homer Ledford's bluegrass band for a two-week promotion.

This was to be the biggest test of my instincts so far. To my delight, they were right. Most of the items, including bent-twig love seats (which are still incredibly popular today) sold out in a week and became collectors' items. We were an instant hit in Manhattan. New Yorkers got it, loved it, and wanted it!

With that success, other major department stores took notice. Soon, Neiman Marcus had made plans for its buyers to visit Kentucky for boutique items for its posh Beverly Hills store. Then the buyers at Marshall Fields in Chicago showed up. Before long, "Kentucky Country Chic" (a phrase we coined) had become famous.

Everything was going great, but I wasn't about to stop there. I'm a firm believer in thinking as big as possible, and if you're building momentum, keep it going. When my husband and I went on an official state trip to Japan, I carefully packed some pieces to take along. Once there, I made an appointment with the buyers at Japan's second biggest department store, Takashimaya (we now have one on Fifth Avenue in New York). Before the appointment I had no idea if they would appreciate this art. Within the first ten minutes I was getting a good feeling about it because they nodded happily each time I brought out a new item. But I wondered if perhaps they were just being polite.

Then, by the end of the meeting, one of the men asked me if I knew the song "My Old Kentucky Home" by Stephen Foster.

Know it? It's the official state song of Kentucky. It's the song we sing before the big race at the Kentucky Derby each year. "Oh, the sun shines bright on my old Kentucky home," I began to sing. Their faces lit up, and their heads bobbed up and down. It turns out that Stephen Foster, who wrote the words and music, is a folk hero in Japan. Who would have guessed it? A few months later Takashimaya launched a "Made in Kentucky" store promotion featuring Kentucky crafts in Tokyo!

The lesson here: Use your instincts to read other people when you're telling them about your idea. Watch them for a response. Give them a chance to respond. Then don't be afraid to demonstrate your passion for your idea when you discover that they are open to sharing it. And if a song will help, give it a try!

By 1983 the craft industry had exploded. Kentucky—known for its horses, coal, bourbon, and tobacco—was now being hailed as one of the leading craft and folk art centers of America. Whenever I could, whether it was at craft markets or as first lady, I told stories about the lives of the craftspeople and what inspired them. After I was first lady, I wrote two books, *Kentucky Craft: Handmade and Heartfelt* and *Craft in America: Celebrating the Creative Work of the Hand*, detailing their histories and their stories. My passion was ongoing, and so is their work.

In 1992 I took it to the next level: television. Once again, we were told it would never work when we presented the idea to buyers for the QVC shopping network. Everyone at that table looked at each other with eyebrows raised. They could not fathom how selling handmade items would work on television. Not that they didn't like what I showed them. They did. But the whole point of selling on TV, they explained, was to mass-market products that were machine-made and could be sold in volume. At that time the network was successfully selling jewelry, computers, and beauty products. Handmade merchandise would never "move," they said.

Everyone, that is, except the visionary president of QVC, Doug Briggs, who understood the importance of keeping this art alive. He thought consumers would want to purchase these handmade objects. Plus, he liked that it was all made in America. He gave us the go-ahead.

Our first show, *Kentucky Crafts with Phyllis George*, was on the air a few months later. If it was made by hand and we could put it in a box and ship it, we sold it. The governor of Kentucky at the time, Brereton Jones, even taped a segment promoting the state and its craft industry that we aired in mid-show. On the program, I not only talked about the objects, I told stories about the craftspeople. And we sold $375,000 worth of handmade items in two hours! Amazing. And they said it wouldn't work.

Soon we expanded the program to encompass all states and renamed it *American Crafts with Phyllis George*. That show aired three to four times a year for seven years and was so popular that it generated up to $400,000 each hour. Throughout that time I continued telling stories about the people who made these wonderful objects. If you bought Molly Dallas' pottery pieces, you knew how Molly painted the old English spatterware and farmyard animals in blue and white. If you ordered a beautiful handmade basket from Bradford Baskets of Troy, Pennsylvania, you'd learn exactly the amazing process by which they were woven.

Previously, those artists had shown their work in local markets and a few small galleries, and each would be thrilled to sell a few a year. Over those seven years, we sold close to $20 million worth of crafts on TV. The show was a huge boost for the craftspeople of America. These artists, many of whom had previously considered abandoning their work, not only gained recognition and respect, but they could boost their family's income and continue with their art. Our efforts also helped generate among the American people a broad appreciation and demand for their work that continues to sustain the craft movement today and into the future.

Today the American craft business is a $4 billion industry. Kentucky alone generates $50 million.

I also remain a faithful collector. After nearly a decade on the craft show circuit I had accumulated tons of craft and folk art, including over thirty hand-carved Uncle Sam figures, a hundred quilts, thirty walking sticks, several Shaker rockers, and dozens upon dozens of baskets. And I have passed many down to my children. Every year since my daughter was born, I've given her a quilt as a Christmas gift. Each year I've also given my son hand-carved pieces of folk art, representing figures like Abraham Lincoln, Daniel Boone, Elvis Presley, and a Kentucky basketball player. Hopefully, they will pass these treasures on to their children.

The effect of trusting my instincts on American craft has been widespread and long-lasting. It is one of the most rewarding things I've done in my life.

Trusting your instincts is basically about knowing and trusting yourself. Now when I tell my family, friends, and business associates that I have a gut instinct about something, they say, "Listen to her." *You can use your instincts to help yourself and others as well.*

Lesson

6

KEEP YOUR
OPTIONS OPEN

When I moved back to New York six years ago, I found myself at a crossroads. My beloved father had died recently, and after almost two decades living in Kentucky I was separated from my husband, John. Our divorce was pending. It was a time for endings but also a time for beginnings. I had a lot of decisions to make.

Like most women starting over, I was confused and hesitant at first. Where should I go? What should I do? I could stay in Kentucky, where people knew me as Phyllis George Brown, the governor's wife. I could return to Texas, where people knew me as Phyllis Ann, the girl they grew up with. Or I could come back to New York, where I could be anyone I wanted to be. *If you're in search of new options, go where you will find the most.* For me, that was New York, so I took the plunge, made the decision, and became Phyllis George again.

My experience and that of my friends has taught me that *you maximize your chances for success and happiness if if you keep your options open. That means two things. First, when you develop any plan, don't limit yourself to only one option. Allow for a number of possibilities. That way, if plan A doesn't work, you can go to plan B. If plan B doesn't work, you can go to plan C. Second, no matter how confident you are about making a plan, don't discount the role of chance. Always remain open to options you haven't even considered.*

∾

Once I was back in New York, I had more decisions to make. I found a new place to live, but what about a new career? What were my options? Hour after hour I sat in my new tenth-floor apartment overlooking the treetops of Central Park, trying to visualize what I wanted to do and be in my new life. *Visualize your dream. Paint a picture in your mind as a useful first step when entering a new phase of life. Imagine yourself in various settings and different roles. What feels right? Then see yourself in that environment. Does it seem comfortable to you?*

As you think through the possibilities, ask yourself: *What have I learned in previous situations that can help me now? This is key because new options are often variations on or combinations of old ones.*

When I began to visualize my options, I thought about the skills I had cultivated in earlier situations and analyzed what had worked for me before. So I wrote down the following:

—*Go back to television*. I had a great deal of television experience after my years at CBS, plus hosting five Rose Bowl parades; cohosting, judging, and performing at eight Miss America pageants; and reporting from three Super Bowls.

—*Write another book*. I had written two full-color coffee table books on the subject of American craft, and I could be interested in doing more.

—*Pursue acting*. I had over three years of acting lessons and had done dozens of commercials, so I could go back into this arena.

—*Start another business*. I know I have entrepreneurial skills, so I could launch another company as I did with Chicken by George.

—*Go back to sportscasting*. I had already established myself as a professional sportscaster and could look for new opportunities in that area.

—*Lecture*. I had experience speaking to many different types of groups, especially as Miss America and first lady, and enjoyed interacting with the public.

—*Work for children's and women's issues*. I had done a lot of work with Save the Children, and creating a full-time job in this area was of great interest to me.

Not bad options! Not bad at all.

Although I was examining my options as a mature woman with many life experiences behind me (more on that in a moment), this recent situation reminded me of when I first moved to New York in my early twenties. ***History does repeat itself!*** At that time, I put broadcast journalism at the top of my list of career goals; acting was second. Other possibilities I list-ed were singing, dancing, and modeling. I had experience with them all, and I wasn't going to rule out any possibility.

I used my Miss America scholarship money for classes in speech and diction. To prepare for jobs in broadcasting, I went from saying "jist," "git," "nite," and "rite" in my Texas drawl to enunciating more clearly "just," "get," "night," and "right." I also studied acting, singing, and dancing, trying to learn anything I thought could broaden my career prospects. If I had studied only acting and didn't get any parts, I would have had nothing to fall back on. Instead, I tried to prepare for numerous things. I didn't close any doors. ***When you're starting out, it's important not to dismiss any alternatives. What you want to be and what you become may be two different things.***

On auditions I was open to anything. If booking agents had asked, "Phyllis, can you dance and play the harmonica at the same time?" my answer would have been "Absolutely." Had they asked, "Can you swan dive off the high diving board?" my answer would have been "Of course." If they would just let me in the door, I knew I could learn what was needed to do the job. I was entering the working world for the first time, and I lacked the professional experience that would help me later in life. However, I did have the exuberance of youth and the belief that I could do pretty much anything.

It's amazing what comes your way when you keep your options open. Television broadcasting was my primary career goal, but because of my acting lessons, I'd gotten jobs appearing in commercials for major brands. Those jobs helped me pay the rent until I got my first regular job. My big opportunity came when I auditioned for the role of cohost of *Candid Camera*. Everyone was surprised when Allen Funt offered the job to me. It was doubly remarkable to me because I would be not only the show's very first cohost, but the first *female* cohost! Still, was it my first choice? Not really. Was I going to turn it down? No way. Knowing I wasn't going to be offered a broadcast position at one of the networks or a starring role in a feature film, I decided to accept! After all, this was a paying job on a popular show. Because I had prepared myself in so many different areas, I felt confident I could do it.

After a year of cohosting *Candid Camera*, to my surprise, CBS Sports offered me a job. Again, I took it because it seemed a good opportunity and I felt confident that I could learn to do it well. But it wasn't as if being a sportscaster had been on my list of goals. In fact, there were virtually no women in national sportscasting at the time, so such a job wouldn't have occurred to me.

Much later, after I had moved to Kentucky and left national television, a family friend suggested I go into the chicken business. My first thought was, "Are you kidding?" Like sportscasting, starting my own business—let alone a chicken company—had never been on my career radar screen. But I decided to take it on, and I was pleased to help make Chicken by George a success.

What did these three experiences have in common? I had never sat down and written any of them on a professional goals list. In fact, I was the first woman to take on each one. I have a good imagination, but not that good! The idea for each came from someone else. They approached me; I was glad I was prepared and said yes.

Be open to any opportunity that comes your way—even if you never thought of it as an option. Understand that you don't always have to be the one initiating new options; you might be the perfect fit for someone else's plan without even knowing it yet!

Cathleen Black, who is now president of Hearst Magazines, learned that lesson on her way to becoming one of the most accomplished and powerful women in newspaper and magazine publishing. Cathie has been my friend since I interviewed her on the *CBS Morning News* in my Women of Influence series. She is now head of a $1.5 billion publishing empire that includes *Good Housekeeping, O, Cosmopolitan, Esquire, Town and Country*, and eleven other magazines. For the past four years, *Forbes* has ranked her among the top thirty "most powerful women in American business." But Cathie says that when she graduated from college with an English degree, she applied for an executive training program at an advertising agency and was told it was for men only. After pounding the pavement for a while, she was finally offered a position as an assistant in advertising sales at *Holiday* magazine. "I didn't have a clue what advertising sales even meant at the time," Cathie says. But she sensed that succeeding in the job would depend more on results than on gender, so she took it.

Years later that small position had led Cathie to a high-flying job as publisher of *New York* magazine. "I loved it, it was prominent, the magazine was hot, and we broke news every Monday," she says. "It was verrrry exciting."

Then, in 1982, out of the blue came a call from an executive headhunter. Some people from outside New York were going to launch a national newspaper and wanted to talk to her about a job. Like anyone operating in the media capital of the world, Cathie admits to being skeptical. "They were so *not* New Yorkers," she remembers. "They were kind of … small town. I thought, They're gonna launch this newspaper in major markets across the country?!" Still, she agreed to a meeting and had a good conversation with them. Cathie left it thinking, "This newspaper is going to be really big and important. But there was not a person in New York City or in Washington, DC, who gave it an iota of a chance for success. 'If it's not the *New York Times*, if it's not the *Wall Street Journal*,' they'd say, 'then who could need it?'"

Many, many people, it turned out, because the newspaper was *USA Today*, which would go on to become one of the most successful newspapers in the country. But the launch got off to a slow start, and in the spring of 1983 Cathie got another call. "The newspaper was about nine months old and hemorrhaging red ink," she says. "They hadn't been able to sell a page of advertising, but they still had this gigantic dream." They wanted to talk to her again.

First, they offered her the presidency of Gannett Media Sales, which involved their cross-media companies. Throughout three meetings she kept telling them the job was not for her. Then, after one more meeting, they asked her to become president of *USA Today*. And suddenly it all made sense.

"I walked out of my office at *New York* magazine," she recalls, "and there was a white stretch limo outside. I got into the limo all by myself, we went to La Guardia to the private aircraft terminal, I got into the Gannett airplane all by myself, and I flew to Washington to change my life! I had two thoughts: one, I was like Dorothy going to Oz. And second, I was literally pinching myself and saying, for a girl from the south side of Chicago, this ain't at all bad! I felt like a pioneer."

Cathie took a chance in moving from a successful job to one that was completely new. But she was strong-willed and confident enough to welcome a new option that unexpectedly came her way. She says about it today, "It was an amazing experience, very difficult, very challenging, but I wouldn't change it for a minute."

Be flexible. *Insisting that life has to follow one predetermined plan is a recipe for stress and frustration. Opening yourself to a surprise can yield unanticipated rewards.*

~

Cathie's success in taking advantage of an unexpected opportunity contrasts with the experience of another of my dear friends, the world-famous novelist Barbara Taylor Bradford. Ten of Barbara's eighteen best-selling books have been made into movies, and over 63 million copies of her books have been sold in 39 languages in 89 countries. Barbara had one dream early in life, but she only reached it after several detours along the way. As a result, she learned an important lesson: *It's never too early or too late to try a new option. Some may say you're too young for a job; others will say you're too old to make a change. If you're convinced you're ready, don't listen. Only you will know whether a particular opportunity is right for you.*

Growing up in Leeds, England, Barbara recalls overhearing her grandmother say to her mother, "You're giving Barbara too many grand ideas." She also remembers her mother's response: "I'm teaching her to reach for the stars, and maybe she'll get the moon."

The young Barbara always had a love for words and writing. When one of her stories was published in a children's magazine when she was ten, she decided on her career goal: "When I grew up," she resolved, "I was going to write books." But if writing books was plan A, Barbara would have to go through plans B and C first. Thinking she couldn't be a novelist until she had lived life a bit, she decided to become a journalist and got a job on the *Yorkshire Evening Post*. After that, she moved to London, where she became a writer for the fashion department of a women's magazine. A year later, when she wanted to leave to find a newspaper job, her editor said she was too young. "She insisted that a twenty-one-year-old would never get a job on a London newspaper," Barbara recalls. Fortunately, she didn't listen. "I left the magazine with a smile on my face: I already had a job. On the *London Evening News*."

But in spite of her progress as a journalist, Barbara had never forgotten her early ambitions. She married and moved to New York, where she wrote a syndicated column on decorating and design. Then she did start writing books, but they were on interior design. After six of them, she thought again of her initial plan A. "I never lost my desire to write a novel," she says. "I dreamed about it. And one day I decided to talk to the head of the publishing house which published my nonfiction books."

But she was ahead of others in recognizing her ability to take on this new option, and the publisher was astonished that she wanted to write fiction. "What makes you think you can do it?" she remembers him saying to her. "It's a difficult job, requires a lot of talent. You'll never get a novel off the ground. Forget it. Stick to writing decorating books."

Barbara says she was "thrown by his comments for a while. But I eventually bounced back and started four different novels over a period of time. When I had the idea for *A Woman of Substance*, I completed an outline and 192 pages and chose not to send it to that particular publisher. I sent it to an editor at Doubleday whom I knew."

"I guess I proved that somewhat disdainful publisher wrong and my mother right," she says with delight today. "I never stopped reaching for the stars. That first novel, *A Woman of Substance*, stayed on the *New York Times* best-seller list for fifteen months!"

~

Like Barbara, I learned it was never too late to try something new when, six years ago, I considered the options I wrote on my list for this new phase of my life. Here's what I did.

The book option moved to the top of the list when I was approached by a publisher who knows I'm a collector of quilts and the author of two books on American craft. When he asked me to write an illustrated book on the history of quilts, entitled *Living with Quilts*, I jumped at the chance to share my passion for quilts with others. For the next few months I busied myself with this labor of love in support of an art form that is dear to my heart.

Then it was on to another option—going back into television—when I was chosen to host the TV version of the popular magazine *Woman's Day*. It was the first time a magazine had been turned into a cable television show, and we developed a wonderful eclectic program that was well received by the media and the audience. That job was very satisfying because it combined broadcasting with some of my top interests: craft, fashion, decorating, health, cooking, women's and children's issues, and celebrity interviews. Everything was going well, when suddenly I was reminded of the importance of keeping more than one option open. A year into the series there was a change in administration at Hachette Fillipachi in America, the corporate parent of *Woman's Day*. The CEO who had championed our show left to head another company. The new CEO didn't have the same commitment and decided he didn't want the magazine to continue in the television business. In spite of the show's popularity, it was canceled.

At that point, I again discovered that ***timing is everything***. Out of the blue, a top New York casting agent, Ellen Chenoweth, called to invite me to audition for a feature film, *Meet the Parents*. Why had she called? It's a funny story that illustrates the value of keeping your options open, and never being afraid to try something new, *and* always staying in touch with your longtime friends, who may be the very ones who bring you new options.

Earlier that year, my close friend Charles had thrown a fiftieth birthday party for me and eighty friends from all over the country. One of the guests was producer Jane Rosenthal (whom you read about in Chapter 3), a longtime pal whom I'd gotten to know back when I was on *The NFL Today*.

The birthday party was an elegant affair held at the Columbus Citizens Foundation, a magnificent historic mansion turned into a private club on New York's Upper East Side. After dinner, it was time for entertainment.

"Tonight," I began, standing before the illustrious crowd, "I have a surprise for you." This was a special treat for me because when I was growing up, my girlfriends and I used to go out into our garage and put on the record from the musical *Gypsy*. We would pretend we were famous Broadway performers as we danced and sang along with the songs. (We never really grow up, do we?)

This night I'd arranged for two wonderful Broadway actresses to perform songs from *Gypsy*. My friend Mary Testa played Mazeppa, the one with a bugle, and Anna McNeely played Electra, the one whose costume lit up in the most private of parts. Then, when the music started, to everyone's astonishment, I came out singing and dancing as Tessie Tura, the ballet dancer. In front of this distinguished group—which included Governor George Pataki, Barbara Walters, Donald Trump, Paula Zahn, Deborah Norville, Liz Smith, Cathie Black, Barbara Taylor Bradford, and other friends and family—we three did a rendition of my favorite song from the play.

"Ya gottta get a gimmmickkkk!" I belted out as I was bumping and grinding in a black gown with a long red chiffon scarf. Everyone cheered (they couldn't believe it!). However, my kids looked horrified. But I thought, It's my party and I'll sing and dance if I want to! You only turn fifty once. Plus, I knew I'd never make it to Broadway, so this moment, in front of a captive audience, was my chance to have a little fun!

It was a bit of a shocker to see Miss Straitlaced Phyllis up there singing the stripper song. But it was also an eye-opener for everyone, including Jane, who remembered my performance (if you want to call it that!) when she began casting for *Meet the Parents*. She told the casting agent to call me, and I auditioned along with the other women trying out for the role. Three weeks went by, and I hadn't heard a word. So I figured one of the more experienced actresses had gotten the part. Then, on a Saturday afternoon, I got a call from Jane. "Phyllis," she said, "how would you like to be in a movie?" I almost fell out of my chair. I got the part! Plan C had arrived from out of nowhere. On Monday, I was on the set as a working actress.

I learned two lessons from this experience. *First, patience is a virtue—and I don't have it. But I'm working on it! If you force things and push too hard, you'll get frustrated. But if you're patient, it will come naturally. Second, new options can come from anywhere. So put yourself in positions that may attract opportunities to you. Get out. Be seen. Tell your friends. Let people know what you can do and what you're willing to try. The more you share with them, the more likely they are to think of you when a new possibility arises.*

After finishing *Meet the Parents*, it was on to plan D. I developed inspirational speeches based on the "never say never" ideas that are in this book. For a year I traveled around the country, delivering addresses to all kinds of groups, from chambers of commerce to women's clubs, to being a keynote speaker at a number of big conventions and seminars. I became a master at combining these trips with taking care of my responsibilities as a mother and daughter: commuting back and forth to Kentucky, where my daughter was finishing high school; to Texas, where my mother still lives; to Pennsylvania, where my son was in college.

At the end of that year I was able to try out another option on my list when my friend Richard Kirshenbaum (whom you read about in Chapter 4) approached me about a new business venture. I've known Richard for twenty years, ever since his start-up agency, Kirshenbaum and Bond, took on the ad campaign for Chicken by George. His eye-popping TV commercial played on the fact that I was the first woman to compete with the "big boys" in the chicken world, Frank Perdue and Don Tyson. For that ad, wearing an elegant, off-the-shoulder, black evening gown, I descended a grand staircase in a gorgeous Beverly Hills home and spoke directly to Frank and Don. "Hey, boys," I said, "wait until you see *my* chicken breasts!" (The making of that ad, by the way, was filmed by *20/20* to illustrate how an ad campaign for a start-up company like ours is developed. When our segment aired on the show, I was in negotiations with Hormel to sell the company to them, and the publicity convinced Hormel to finalize the deal. Again, ***timing is everything!***)

Now Richard and I are working together on a new line of beauty products. This new option is ideal for me because it draws on my previous experience as a businesswoman and a "BQ" (beauty queen). ***See how one thing leads to another, even if they are years apart!***

When something is meaningful to you, you can reinvent it in new ways. You can always make something old new again.

Lesson

7

FEEL THE POWER OF BEING NICE

Now, I ain't no Miss Goody Two-Shoes, but I was brought up to be a nice girl and being nice hasn't hurt me. In fact, I've learned that being nice is a powerful commodity. Today it seems that almost everywhere you look, it's considered entertaining to discover people's flaws and make fun of their weaknesses. In such an atmosphere, some people have come to think "nice" is a bad word. They're the ones who believe that old cliché "nice guys finish last," and if you want to be successful, you can't be nice at the same time. Some just don't deal in nice talk. They define nice as the opposite of powerful, strong, and important. To them, being nice is a sign of weakness. I'm here to tell you that way of thinking is a big mistake!

Being nice shows that you're comfortable with yourself, that you're strong and confident enough to reach out to others, that you're not afraid to show your interest in them or share your genuine concern. The key to "nice power" is simple—imagine yourself as the other person. Think: How would it feel if someone said or did that to me? If I were in his or her situation, what would make me feel better? If I were facing what she or he is, what would I want someone to do for me? It takes a secure person to treat everyone you meet the same way—with kindness and respect.

There's a connection between being nice and being friendly, but they're not exactly the same thing. Being nice means that you are polite; you are courteous; you are considerate of others' feelings. Being friendly means that you extend the same warmth to everyone that you do to your friends. Being friendly is the more outgoing aspect of being nice.

When I first moved to New York from Texas in the 1970s, people told me I was different because I was nice *and* friendly! I'd get into a cab and start talking with the driver. In a restaurant, I'd strike up a conversation with the waiter. In stores, I couldn't believe how rude some of the salesclerks could be; I thought they were supposed to help—after all, I'm the customer! But I still tried to be "nice and friendly." Some New Yorkers were suspicious of my friendliness, although a lot of them complimented me for it. If I was told once, I was told a hundred times: You are *so refreshing*! I got totally sick of hearing that word. I began to think that I needed to adopt more aloof ways so that I would fit in. In other words, I tried to develop an "Attitude." After a trial run, however, I realized *you can't be something you're not*. It's about keeping a good attitude, not having an "Attitude." My outgoing spirit was too ingrained in me to change. Soon I started to see how these qualities were working *for* me, not against me.

Since then I've put being nice to work in all kinds of situations. When I got my small role in the movie *Meet the Parents* two years ago, I was thrilled by the prospect of getting to work with Robert De Niro and Ben Stiller, two great actors from two different generations, who were playing the leads. If I was on the set with them every day, I figured, I would have the chance to talk with them. I didn't think we'd necessarily become bosom buddies, but as working actors, I assumed we'd be friendly and get to know each other a bit. When I mentioned this to a couple of friends, they laughed. Apparently, both men have reputations for not being very talkative and being so focused on their work that it's not easy to engage them in casual conversation. *Well!* Hearing that made me more determined. So I decided, by the time the movie wrapped up, that I was going to get to know those two guys better. *If you had such a chance, wouldn't you be determined to take advantage of it?*

So when I first met Ben Stiller, I said, "It's really nice to meet you, Ben. How are you?" and he said, "Fine." Later I made a few remarks about how hard he had been working on the film, and he said, "Uh-huh." He was polite but not forthcoming. Still, I didn't think he was unfriendly; he was just preoccupied with his work. After all, I reminded myself, he's one of the stars, and although I had had success in other areas, I was still a new kid on the block when it came to the movies. I didn't take it personally.

I kept speaking to him every day, saying things like "Hi, Ben, how are you? Great job on that scene at the pool." I'd comment on a scene we'd completed or ask how he thought things were going. Since he was clearly focused on making the movie, I generally stuck to that subject. Over time he began to respond more and more and seemed to warm up to me. The process was helped when his beautiful fiancée, Christine Taylor, visited the set, and I got to meet her too. Somehow, by the end of the filming, we'd become comfortable enough with each other that I was suggesting wedding coordinators for their upcoming big event. Now they're married and have a little girl.

For De Niro, the clincher was discovering we had a common interest. One day the director called a break in the filming to check the blocking and camera position, but he told the cast not to leave the set because we'd resume filming soon. So everybody found the closest seat in the living room area and plopped down, but somehow I was left without a place to sit. Bob was in back in this big club chair with an ottoman, and he motioned for me to come over and sit next to him.

So I headed for the ottoman. When I got settled, I asked him who he liked in the upcoming Super Bowl. It turns out he's a football fan, so we starting talking about sports. Our conversation felt very comfortable. It was funny because when we went back to the scene, everyone was asking me what we talked about. It seems a lot of people are in awe of him because he's such a legend. "We were talking about sports," I answered. "Leave it to you to find the right topic," they all laughed.

For the remaining weeks of the filming Bob and I had a number of conversations, some short and some longer. When at the end of one day he said, "Bye, Phyl." He called me by my nickname! I knew I'd really broken through.

Now, I certainly wouldn't claim I became great pals with these guys, but I enjoyed spending time talking with them. Would it have been easier to sit back and not try to get to know them? Absolutely. But I like meeting new people; it makes my life more interesting. Throughout my life, being friendly and reaching out to people around me have opened up new avenues for me. It's part of what comes from being nice.

I'd already seen one small example of this when I became Miss America. The day after I won, the *Atlantic City Press* carried a story about how the doormen and policemen at the Atlantic City Convention Center and the bellman in my hotel were all pulling for me. They appreciated that I always said hello, asked how they were doing, and thanked them for being there. They had hoped I would win because they thought I was so *nice*! I was flattered and surprised because it's simply not my nature to walk past people without nodding and smiling. I'd always taken this for granted, but it seems others didn't.

My parents had taught me when I was growing up that being nice was part of having good manners. Be polite; say please and thank you; if you can't say something nice about someone, don't say anything at all. If I had disagreements with anybody—girls talking behind your back, that kind of thing—I'd just walk away. Don't kid yourself: I can get ticked off! But I always tried to remain friendly and avoid hurting anyone's feelings.

Of course, there was that other definition of "nice." Nice girls, as my parents also reminded me, didn't get drunk, behaved like a lady, and were always home before midnight. Getting home early was not a problem in Denton, Texas, where a night on the town meant driving up and down the main strip and stopping at the Sonic, where the servers roller-skated out to the car.

And of course, times are different now. Recently I've been saddened to read that many teenagers today think it's funny to be mean to others, saying and doing cruel things to hurt others, starting whisper campaigns, using Web sites to spread hateful rumors. I realize that I grew up in a more innocent time and that the moral compass today for young people is different. Each generation has to adapt to its times, but the basics of respecting other people never change. ***All of us who are*** *parents have an important role in teaching our children when they're young about good values and good manners.*

Those lessons stick with us and serve as a guide when we make decisions on our own later in our lives. In New York, I took the lessons from my earlier years in Texas with me. At one point, I had accepted a job with talk show host and producer David Susskind to do interviews for a new television show based on *People* magazine. It was one of the first magazine-style shows on TV, and the position was a career opportunity for me. However, I found Susskind to be a rather complicated man who had a real edge to him. Soon it was clear that the job was not a good fit. The directors' idea of a good story was following the ever-reclusive Greta Garbo around with hidden cameras, trying to get shots of this woman known for saying "I want to be alone." She had not given an interview in years, and I thought they were invading her privacy. On what was supposed to be a legitimate magazine show, I couldn't see how this was a justifiable way to go about developing a story.

It got worse from there. I remember sitting in one meeting with all the staff when Susskind said he wanted me to do more gossip-style stories. He was particularly convinced that I should do one on a popular singer-actress and her problems with drugs and men. As someone who had been taught to be fair and to give people the benefit of the doubt, I told them I couldn't do the story because it included no interviews with her and showed only one side of her life. Doing it their way didn't seem to be legitimate journalism to me. He immediately called my manager and complained. But I had principles, and I knew this kind of reporting might be right for someone else, but not for me. My lawyer had to get involved. "You're not going to turn her into a gossip queen," he told them. "She's a broadcast journalist."

The show was soon canceled—doomed by a number of things, including poor scheduling since it aired opposite *Monday Night Football* at its peak in popularity and thus competed with my sports audience. Still, it was a useful learning experience because it helped me see two things. First, I could work only in a situation that I felt was consistent with my principles. I couldn't put my head on the pillow at night if I wasn't content with who I was and what I was doing. Second, I needed to learn how to speak up for myself while staying within my own comfort zone.

A problem with being known as someone who is upbeat and positive is that sometimes they want you to just smile, look pretty, and not open your mouth. Translation: We don't care what you have to say or your opinion; we just want you to light up the screen. Fortunately, that's changed now, but it happened a lot early in my career.

Well, thank you for thinking I'm pretty and thank you for saying I have a great smile—but hey, let me tell you what I *think*! I *do* have a brain, and I have opinions.

Until I turned fifty, I often had a hard time speaking up. But, let me tell you: *If you don't speak up for yourself, no one else will. But there's a way to do it that will be constructive rather than destructive and will lead to a more positive outcome. It's what I call PNP: Positive, Negative, Positive. You "sandwich" what you have to say that's critical or unfavorable between two positives.* Starting off and ending with something good cushions the negative part and makes it much easier for the recipient to hear. It works every time. Let me give you a couple of examples.

Someone asks you to a party, and either you can't go or you just don't want to go. Maybe you've never enjoyed going to that person's house, but you don't necessarily want him or her to know that. So instead of flatly turning the person down with an instant "no," say something like this: "Thank you so much for the invitation. But I have something else already scheduled for that evening, so I won't be able to make it. I'm sure everyone there will have fun and I hope you'll invite me some other time." That was positive—then negative—then positive.

Or say you're not happy with the performance of one of your staff members. He's getting sloppy and not turning in good work anymore, but you're convinced he's capable of doing better. Instead of calling him in and immediately berating him, try the following: "You know, Alex, I've been pleased with the progress you've made in your job. You're really contributing to the team here. But there's one area that I'd like to see you work on that will enable you to make an even greater contribution." Then discuss the specific area that needs improvement. After that, close the meeting with: "Alex, I'm so glad we had this conversation. I'm confident in your ability to make these changes." Again, the negative part of the conversation is softened by placing it in a positive framework.

Tickle, *slap*, *tickle*, as one of my friends called it. **When you have something negative to say to someone, help the other person feel good about herself or himself first. That person will then be prepared to respond in a productive way to the "negative" part of the conversation. He or she will be less likely to get defensive and reject what you have to say. Rather than thinking of you as critical and uncaring, that person will think of you as being helpful and nice.**

Learn to use the power of words. The way you say something has a tremendous impact on people—whether you're delivering bad news, giving constructive criticism, or speaking up for yourself. Think of it as **saying no with a gift**. If you're not able to say yes to the other person, use the power of being nice and give the person something that makes him or her feel good anyway.

Another lesson I've learned from dealing with the difficult situations described elsewhere in this book: ***Always take the high road***. If someone treats you unkindly, don't retaliate by getting down and wallowing in the mud with that person! ***If you feel you could kill them, kill them with kindness.*** It will make you feel better and stronger because you've shown you're able to rise above it. When you take the high road, it will surprise the other person. Believe me, they're waiting for any excuse to take another swing at you. Not only that: When you refuse to wallow with them, they will be robbed of the chance to say something negative about you. And who knows: you may need them in the future for something, so don't burn your bridges.

Learning to be gracious when you've been rejected can even open up new opportunities for you, as my longtime special friend Mary Hart discovered. Mary has been the popular cohost of television's *Entertainment Tonight* for an amazing twenty years. Mary is also one of the nicest people I know, and I'm convinced that her niceness—along with her talent and willingness to take risks—helped her progress from being a teacher in South Dakota to being a nationally popular entertainment journalist.

Mary got her start when a brand-new cable company in her home state called one day with an offer to do a talk show. As a former Miss South Dakota, she'd been a guest on talk shows but had never really considered it a career option. Still, she says, "The second I sat down to do my first on-air interview, I knew that was what I wanted to do." After success there, she moved on to Oklahoma City, where she hosted another talk show for three and a half years before deciding to move to Hollywood and test her ability to make it in California. Of course, people all along the way were telling her she would never be able to make it, but she simply used those doubts as a challenge. Though it took almost a year to find a job in Hollywood, one of her auditions finally panned out, and she was chosen to cohost *PM Magazine*, a syndicated program in Los Angeles. Eventually, Regis Philbin invited her to join him as cohost for a national NBC talk show, and in Mary's words, "Things were rolling along glowingly."

Her excitement was short-lived, however. "We were on top of the world," she says, "then, *boom*, four months later, we're canceled. We were off the air. I was out of work again. It was complete deflation. I felt like I was starting all over again. And this time maybe with a little more difficulty because the expectations and excitement level had been very high. And to have everybody supposedly so excited about the talk show and then have the rug pulled out from under you was not a good feeling."

Mary was sitting around feeling discouraged about her career when a phone call came in that made her feel even worse. "This upstart show called *Entertainment Tonight* had just gone on the air, and to add insult to injury, they called and said, 'We know your show was just canceled. Do you mind talking to us about what it feels like to be canceled?'"

It would have been understandable for Mary to say no and turn them away. But she decided to be gracious instead. "I said, 'Well, sure, c'mon over to my humble little abode,' which at that time was a small one-bedroom apartment. So they came over and we talked about it," she says. The next day, to her surprise, "the producers of the show called me and said, 'We think you would fit in very well over here.'" She started out as a correspondent and was later named host.

Mary has just celebrated her twentieth anniversary with the show, and I was pleased recently to present her with a prestigious Gracie Award from American Women in Radio and Television for her outstanding work in television. With her talent, integrity, and warm personality, Mary has become one of the most trusted figures on American television.

Be nice to other people even when you're hurting inside.

Using the power of being nice helps smooth the way for virtually all social situations. My dad always used to say to me, "Phyllis, you never meet a stranger." Yes, I'm an extrovert, but I've also learned techniques for interacting comfortably and successfully with people that anyone can use.

For some reason, for instance, I've never had a problem with a situation that many people find terrifying: walking into a roomful of strangers. Perhaps it's just that I was forced to do it so much early in my career that I had to figure out ways to make it work. The key is to understand that this isn't a test; it's an opportunity. Who knows who you might meet? Someone who can help your career, or become a new friend, or give you some information that will help you with a decision you have to make.

Most people are self-conscious when they walk into a room, but remember that **shyness is a state of mind**. A lot of successful people are naturally shy or fear they're not good at small talk, but they've mastered the art of meeting other people. So don't feel you're alone. If you think you're going to have a panic attack, take several deep breaths before you enter. That will calm you.

When you walk into a room with people who are unfamiliar to you, don't try to meet a crowd. All you need is one person to talk to. Look for the friendliest person you see. Just walk right up, say "Hi, I'm ...," and stick out your hand and smile. I guarantee they'll smile back and introduce themselves.

If you're thinking "Then what?" here are some ideas. Most people like to talk about themselves, so ask them some questions. I always like to ask people where they're from. It's a question that works anytime, anywhere, and it almost always gives you something you can respond to in order to get the conversation rolling. You can also ask what kind of business people are in, or about their families or children, what they're doing at this meeting or event, where they're staying, and so on. Look for common elements. Use the conversation to build your confidence, to get your adrenaline going.

Once you start talking to one person, others will respond to your confidence and will naturally gravitate to you. Remember that many people will be feeling the same as you: nervous about meeting new people, afraid they won't have anything to say. They'll be *grateful* to you for taking the initiative.

And when you meet someone new, repeat that person's name two or three times shortly after you hear it for the first time. "So, Michael, where are you from?" "What kind of business are you in, Michael?" "Michael, so nice to meet you." That will help you remember their names. It's advice you've probably heard before, but it really works.

From the time I was Miss America through my years in politics and sports and the chicken business, there have been countless times I've walked into rooms where I didn't know a soul, and these techniques have never failed me. And if you think for one minute that I have an advantage you might not have because people have seen me on TV or think they recognize me from somewhere else, banish that thought from your head! You have to say to yourself over and over: ***These people should be happy to talk to me because I have something to offer them***. I've also learned the best way to deal with that embarrassing moment when someone rushes up to you with great delight, greets you warmly by name, and then says, "Remember me?" And you don't. There may be times when it works to claim you do and try to fake it. But if you fake it, they may respond, "What's my name?" (I hate that!)—and then you're caught. In most cases, I've found it's better to be honest and say, with a smile in your voice, "Oh, forgive me, can you help me out?" or "Can you place yourself for me?" Then, when they explain, you can say, "Of course," with genuine enthusiasm.

～

Now just in case you're feeling a little nauseated by all of this "nice" talk, let me reassure you about something. One day I'm going to be out promoting this book and I'll meet one of you reading this now and I'll be a little moody. I may be preoccupied with something else on my mind or just not be "on" that day. Like everyone else, I have my bad days. Sometimes I'm not in the right mindset, or I don't feel I have the right "voice" to get out there and be with other people. Some days I get up in the morning and think "I don't feel like being 'Phyllis George' today." On a really bad day I'll have crawled back under the covers and not left my apartment if I'm in one of those "moods." But try to remember we all have those days.

I'm happy to lead the drive for making "nice" a good word again. I've been noticing I'm not the only one. Attorney Ron Shapiro is using his book *The Power of Nice* as the basis for corporate negotiation seminars around the country. Some of our biggest actors, like Tom Hanks, Mary Tyler Moore, Tom Cruise, and Michelle Pfeiffer, are known for being very nice people. We're all on the same track, and I know it can take us where we want to go.

There is a power in being nice. It is a quiet power that cultivates a giving spirit and nurtures positive energy.

LIFE ISN'T PERFECT

Life was nearly perfect for me until I reached the fifth grade at Stonewall Jackson Elementary School and wanted to study the flute and join the school band. To my surprise, my parents refused. "I can't?! You won't let me?! Pleeeeze," I begged them. It was the worst thing that had happened to me in my young life.

But they stood firm. "You're already taking piano lessons," they told me. "You don't have time to do both." Well, I was playing Bach, Beethoven, and Chopin, and at eleven I had entered a national recording contest against pianists twice my age and had come in in first place. My parents wanted me to excel at one instrument instead of playing two, and the piano came naturally to me.

To this day, I remember how deflated I was: my first shocking indication that I wasn't always going to get what I want in life and I wasn't always going to be perfectly happy. Nothing, in fact, is *perfectly* anything, I have discovered.

To a lot of people, my grown-up life may seem like a fairy tale, a Cinderella existence. I married a charming prince, lived in a mansion, gave birth to two healthy children (one boy and one girl), and even wore a gold crown! But I had some seriously imperfect moments in my fairy tale, and the truth is I'm glad for them. I remember when Dustin Hoffman accepted his best actor award for *Rain Man* and said, "I'd like to thank those people who kicked me as well as those who kissed me." That resonated with me. ***It's often the hard knocks in life that shape us and make us strong.***

My friend Walter Anderson learned that lesson as a young marine. Walter is now chairman, publisher, and CEO of *Parade* magazine, which is distributed in more than 330 Sunday newspapers and is, with a circulation of 36 million, one of America's most widely read periodicals. Walter is also a national spokesperson for GED, the program that enables high school dropouts to earn equivalency diplomas. This is a cause dear to Walter's heart since he earned a GED while in the Marine Corps, having dropped out of high school in 1961 to enlist. Later, he went on to gain a college education, write four books, and serve as the editor of *Parade* for twenty years before becoming publisher. I recently had the pleasure of attending a party celebrating his twenty-five years at *Parade*.

But it was in the service that Walter learned to conquer negative thinking. "One day when I was a young marine stationed at Camp Lejeune in North Carolina," he says, "my hands were crushed in an accident. The doctors had to wait a few days for the swelling to subside before they were able to discover whether I had movement or feeling in my fingers. 'Try to move the first finger of your right hand,' the doctor instructed me. As he suggested, I tried, but nothing happened. 'I can't,' I told him, and he said we'd try again tomorrow."

But Walter's platoon sergeant, who was present at the time, had another idea. "'Wait just a minute,' he interrupted. 'Move the first finger of your right hand *now*!' he ordered me. I struggled. The finger moved."

"I've thought of that experience occasionally over the years," Walter says, "whenever, from time to time, I've heard myself or someone else promise to *try* to achieve a goal." In fact, today he traces being prepared for that moment much earlier, in boot camp at Parris Island, South Carolina, when he and his fellow recruits had to conquer "the Confidence Course," a succession of logs, lines, and muddy water. "What did I learn from shinnying up ropes, leaping onto and over logs?" Walter explains. "The Marine Corps was right to call the test a confidence course and not an obstacle course—because, truly, that was its purpose. 'If I can get over that log, I can do anything.'"

Like moving his finger and conquering the course, Walter learned, "every day, *obstacles are an opportunity to gain confidence. Every time we prevail—if even for a moment— over anxiety, fear of failure, feelings of vulnerability and inferiority, we are not left even. We are not as we were; we are ahead. With each obstacle we conquer, we grow larger.*"

I couldn't agree more. I tell my children all the time, "I hope you have some early disappointments in your life because you need to learn that life isn't perfect." You need that reality check as soon as possible. *USA Today*'s Al Neuharth gave the same advice in his column once. He said he hopes teenagers have disappointments or failures early in life because if it happens for the first time when they get older, it's a real blow and shock to their system. And I thought, A-men!

It's important for parents to help their children accept loss or failure because you can't always cover for them and make things right: it's not healthy or helpful.

My pal Johnny Bench is often called the greatest catcher ever in baseball. His career achievements include winning the National League Most Valuable Player award in 1970 and 1972 and being named "Greatest Catcher of the Century" by sports fans. Johnny was initiated into baseball's Hall of Fame in 1989. But the career of a major league baseball player inevitably includes disappointments as well, and Johnny credits his father with preparing him to deal with those times that weren't so satisfying.

"When I was playing Little League," Johnny says, "I wanted to win every game, and it was a big disappointment to me when we lost." Even as a boy, Johnny says he was so driven to succeed as a batter that he spent hours in his backyard, tossing rocks and pieces of gravel up into the air to hit with his bat. "I would toss up a rock," he says, "hit it, get another, pick it up, and throw it up to hit it again. I would do this over and over."

When his team lost a game, Johnny knew his father was also disappointed but this wise father helped his son to learn to accept the defeat and get beyond it. "After a loss," Johnny recalls, "my dad would say, 'Hey, let's go get a cheeseburger.' It's such a simple thing, really, but it became a treasured tradition for the two of us, and it gave me a way to start getting over each disappointment. Later on, when I began playing professional baseball, I continued the tradition on my own. After each loss, I would go out for a cheeseburger. No matter how frustrated or downright miserable I was, that little treat would improve my feelings. It helped me put the loss behind me and begin planning for the next game." In this way, his father's lesson helped Johnny develop the resilience that is so necessary for success as a professional athlete and indeed in all areas of life.

My first instinct as a mother was always to smooth things over for my kids when they had a problem in school or with a friend. Then I thought, "No, I can be a sounding board for them, but I have to let them fight their own battles and learn from their mistakes." When Lincoln was pitching a baseball game and questioned a call by the umpire that caused his team to lose or when Pamela made a mistake in her piece at a piano recital, I helped them accept those disappointments and grow from them. *Everybody has setbacks and everybody makes mistakes. The key is: If you lose, don't lose the lesson.*

~

As we become adults, we learn to deal with adult-sized failures and disappointments. We must learn also that *there are times when—no matter how hard you try and how much you believe in yourself—it's impossible to succeed and you must know when to bow out.* I know I talk a lot about never giving up, but there are truly times when you are in the wrong place at the wrong time with the wrong people. At those times, it's important to recognize that it's not meant to be, learn from the experience, and move on.

When I took the job of cohosting the *CBS Morning News* in 1984, I had no idea that my new venture was doomed from the start because, as a colleague said to me later, I was miscast. In fact, I thought it was the perfect opportunity. Was I in for a shock!

After ten glorious years I had decided to leave my wonderful job at the highly successful *NFL Today*. I still loved that job, but I was ready for a change. Sportscasting involved so much traveling that I was frequently away from my two young children. Being away from my family on the major holidays during football season was especially hard. Moving to the morning show would enable me to stay in one place and create some normalcy and consistency for Lincoln and Pamela.

Professionally, the job also seemed a challenge that I was ready to tackle. I knew that CBS had been in third place for over thirty years in the morning show lineup. But the executives told me they were going to build the show around me and my personality in an attempt to make it more competitive with ABC's *Good Morning America*, then in first place, and NBC's *Today*, then in second. I believed I could be successful on the kind of show they described. I had been a guest cohost on *Good Morning America*, which had adopted one of the first formats blending news, human interest stories, and entertainment. That combination was a good fit for me, and my appearances there had been well received.

Because I had done so well in the sports division at CBS, I thought when I moved to another division of the same company, I would be welcomed with open arms and treated with the same respect. Sportscasting had been new for me when I first started, but I was given support and time to learn how to use my natural talents, earning the approval of both the executives and the viewers as well as the respect of my colleagues. It seemed realistic to expect the same at the *Morning News*. After all, they were going to pay me close to a million dollars! That was more money than I'd ever dreamed of earning, and it seemed a clear sign of their commitment to me. How could I turn down such an opportunity?

To take the job, I made the necessary adjustments to my life. I moved my family from Kentucky to New York and enrolled Lincoln in prekindergarten. Pamela would be at home with our nanny until I got home each day. John would divide his time between New York, Kentucky, and business travel. I also adjusted my internal and external clocks to get up at 3 a.m. in order to go on air, live, at 7 and greet viewers as they were starting their day.

The expectations were high at the start. The *Washington Post* put me on the cover of its style section with the headline "Phyllis George: CBS's Morning Glory ... She's a Breath of Fresh Air in the Morning." That optimism was echoed almost everywhere by friends, family, and the press alike.

Very soon, however, I realized I was a round peg trying to fit into a square hole. Although the show was competing with more entertainment-driven shows like *GMA*, the *Morning News* was still under the news division at CBS. As a result, the show had long suffered from an identity crisis: Was it news? Was it entertainment? How could it be both and stay true to CBS's hard news tradition? This context made it inherently difficult to transform the morning program into a warm and friendly kind of news show, the kind I would naturally fit into. Of course, I had been told that I was being hired to help make that transition. The execs had promised me that we would be breaking new ground. "It won't be like the hard news shows that we used to do," they'd said. We were going to be competitive in the mornings. I had wanted to get this in writing in my contract, but the attitude from the higher-ups was "Don't worry your pretty little head about it. Trust us!" Even my lawyer reassured me that everything would be okay. *(A lesson in passing: Always get things in writing.)*

But the veterans of the old regime were extremely resistant to change. In somber tones, they reminded me that CBS News was hallowed ground, the home of legendary newsman

Edward R. Murrow. There the news was serious, and it was meant to be taken seriously. And in whispers I heard, *"Phyllis doesn't stand a chance!"*

In fact, a respected former CBS journalist said that, during that period, you'd better walk sideways down the hall so you don't get stabbed in the back. If timing is everything, my timing was off. Here I was, a former Miss America who had been a sportscaster and was married to a popular former governor. From the moment I walked into their hard-edged newsroom with a smile on my face, their resistance to me was obvious. I could feel it. To top it off, the executive producer of the broadcast had been a print journalist but had never produced a TV show.

When you do something that is not right for you, you know it almost immediately. I had no training in hard news, and I admit I made some mistakes on the air. When I did, they were magnified a hundred times. Still, I believed I could grow into the job with time. Despite their promises to me, I thought, if they were determined to keep it a hard news show, I would try my best to make it work.

What I understand now that I didn't then is how hard it is to turn a long-running third-place show around. If it could have been done at all, it would have taken a long, long time— years, not months. Aside from the question of whether I was the right person to try, everyone's expectations, including mine, were unrealistic about the length of time needed to make the show competitive. In the TV business, victory is spelled "R-A-T-I-N-G-S." I was under overwhelming pressure to make a difference, but it couldn't be done overnight.

Yet I continued to try. I wasn't going to run from it. The ratings were somewhat better than they'd been previously, and I was able to do some stories that were a good fit for me. I developed a series called Women of Influence that was right up my alley. But most of the time, my assignments didn't utilize my talents at all. They didn't play to my strengths.

In addition, each day at precisely 8 a.m., I could feel my neck and shoulders knotting up as I sat at the anchor desk. The reason? That was the time our nanny walked Lincoln to school, with Pamela in tow. Lincoln was four, and Pamela was only one. I had visions of them crossing the busy Manhattan streets and cabs jumping the curbs onto the sidewalk and barreling into my babies. I kept thinking that they would be so much happier back in Kentucky where they could run and play in the open space safely.

To make matters worse, sleep became more and more elusive as the months went on. Believe me, the people who do the morning shows deserve medals for working on that schedule day after day, year after year, and always sounding smart and looking fresh at those hours. I needed more hours of sleep than I was getting then to function effectively. Not only was I up at 3 a.m., I was working long hours helping to book people on the show, running out to tape a segment, trying desperately to make the show better. I'd go home and play with the children, have dinner with them, and get them into bed. I'd collapse into bed exhausted and then have trouble falling asleep. Frequently, the show I had prepared for the night before was completely changed by the next morning. I would find a whole new show format shoved under my door to prepare for and deliver on air in a matter of hours. This was another difference from my experience at *Good Morning America*. There we had planned the next day's stories by the early evening, and unless there was a breaking news story, I could sleep like a baby, knowing I was well prepared.

Plus, the media was constantly on my case. I can't count how many discouraging articles I read after the first few months when the honeymoon with the press was over. I was a pioneer female sportscaster and I'd been through political campaigns, so I was used to barbs and criticism. I knew the frustration of having articles written about you that were unfair when you had no comparable platform to defend yourself. But these attacks were personal, and reading mean-spirited cheap shots was especially discouraging because I loved the medium of television so much. I did have some surprising defenders. Former television producer Roger Ailes, now president of Fox, wrote a newspaper column titled: "Stop Trashing Phyllis George." "It's time to stop picking on Phyllis George," he wrote. "Having produced and consulted on talk shows for twenty years I can tell you that even though many Americans think they know how to host a television program and certainly everyone in the press thinks they know how to host one, it's a damn difficult job to do ... she is not a quitter ... this program has been out of control for some time." You never know where your support is going to come from: Ailes was the Republican strategist for John's opponent in the Kentucky governor's race years earlier.

I finally decided to move my children back to Lexington, our home, and I began to commute back and forth. Every weekend, I'd fly to Kentucky to be with them and wind down, then fly back to New York to wind back up again. But the constant going back and forth soon began to take a toll. The stress was getting to me. One time my throat closed up so that I could barely get the words out on camera. I opened my mouth and what emerged was a breathy sound. I was surprised when a writer wrote in *Vogue* magazine, "Who does Phyllis George think she is with that breathy Jackie Kennedy voice?"

I've always had a lot of energy and I can handle a lot at one time, but for the first time in my life I felt my batteries draining. The body is very smart. Mine was clearly trying to flash:

Get out of this place! It's not good for you! I was learning another lesson the hard way: **Everybody has a finite amount of energy and limits to what she or he can do. Listen to your body. It will talk to you if you're willing to listen.**

I kept my game face on, but deep down I knew I was floundering. I was beginning to understand that while I had many strengths as a broadcasting professional, I just didn't have the ones needed for that particular job.

Finally, I realized what a basket case I had become. No one was happy—not me, not my kids, not my husband, not the network. John was contemplating a run for the Senate, and I wanted to be at home more than ever. This was ridiculous. This wasn't right. This had to end.

If you know it's not right, **be willing to walk away with your head held high.**

One day I walked into the office of one of the head honchos at CBS News. He was a very charming, well-liked English gent. "You brought me in to do one kind of show," I said, "but you're still doing it the old way, just with zippier graphics and livelier music. Obviously you want to keep the program a hard news show, and if that's the case, you should hire someone like Maria Shriver. She's worked her whole career as a hard news journalist, and she's great at it." In the transition from old regime to new, I had been caught in the cross fire. He knew it, and I knew it.

After that conversation I left for a much-needed vacation with John on Nantucket and Martha's Vineyard. When we returned, I got a call from my lawyer: CBS and I would mutually agree to part ways and let our lawyers settle the contract.

It was so weird because one day I was there on the show, and the next day I wasn't. Without any explanation to anyone, I was just gone. My loyal assistant, Dee, packed up my things and took them away. Before too long, there was Maria Shriver at the desk, bright and early.

Within a week I'd put my apartment up for sale and was on a flight home to Kentucky. When I pulled into the circular driveway at Cave Hill Place, my old Kentucky home, I finally breathed a sigh of relief. I finally breathed, *period*. I was so relieved to be back in my peaceful, tranquil environment with my children and my husband. There, I could regroup and begin to feel grounded again.

Distance and time are very important in getting over a difficult situation. I had tried and failed, but in the end I learned to be kind to myself. I may have failed at that job, but I wasn't a failure.

When I got home, I wrote in a fury all the things I had wanted to say out loud but never did. I learned that a big part of my stress was that I'd kept my feelings about what was happening bottled up inside; I never complained. Now I know that it is imperative to **have a sounding board. It can be a family member, a friend, or a therapist. But you must discuss your feelings and your frustrations with someone, and not just hold them inside. Learn to let it out in other ways as well. Throw pillows, write it down, take a walk in the park, take a drive in your car and scream at the top of your lungs—whatever works for you.**

Also, a friend gave me a framed copy of the poem "If" by Rudyard Kipling. I sat it on my dressing table and read it over and over each day. Particularly meaningful to me were these lines: "If you can keep your head when all about you / Are losing theirs and blaming it on you, / If you can trust yourself when all men doubt you, / But make allowance for their doubting too." That poem has helped many of my friends as well. I recommend reading it when you're having a hard time. It really helps.

But perhaps the most help came from the therapeutic words of my wise friends. We had lunched with Walter and Betsy Cronkite while we were on vacation at Martha's Vineyard. Walter had helped me not to take my *Morning News* experience so personally. He said when he had hosted the *CBS Morning News* thirty years ago, they hadn't known what they wanted the show to be then and they still didn't. They'd always been in third place.

Other friends in the industry sent me letters filled with positive thoughts and encouragement. Diane Sawyer, whom I'd been hired to replace when she left, wrote to remind me that all women in broadcasting had suffered bruises and that someday I would be able to look back and laugh at what I'd experienced. Jane Pauley, then at *Today*, sent a very funny note and also came to my defense in a speech quoted in the *New York Times*, saying that I was "sabotaged by the ineptitude of CBS. CBS did nothing to make it work for her." Barbara Walters urged me not to think of the experience as a defeat but to look forward to new opportunities.

My friend Charles Kuralt is not with us anymore. I miss him even more when I remember how his note made me laugh. "Welcome to the company of ex–*Morning News* people," he wrote. "We are a very large but distinguished crowd who know the joy of *not* getting up at 3 a.m. A pleasure most people never get a chance to experience. But isn't it wonderful? I may give a party for us all one day—Walter Cronkite, Mike Wallace, Lesley Stahl, Diane Sawyer, and now you get to come!"

It was then I truly, deeply, understood that *you need to lean on your friends and your family during tough times. They will give you unconditional support and love and will help you keep things in perspective.*

As soon as I left the show, words of support even started flowing from the media. "Call me mad, call me crazy," wrote the *Washington Post* television critic, "but I miss Phyllis. She cheered up my mornings." And Howard Stringer (now Sir Howard Stringer), one of the top executives at CBS News at the time, was later quoted as saying that the network had mishandled my appearance. "It was the network's fault," he said. "I don't think we did right by her. She worked very hard and was genuinely likable. If we were going to bring her in, we should have built the show around her. Instead we tried to make her fit our version of the news."

Over time, I was disheartened to see that the women hired after me also became part of the revolving door. We all had hopes, each one of us, that we could make it work. But each of us ultimately realized we couldn't because we weren't the problem—and we couldn't be the solution.

None of that mattered to me anymore. I was on a new path with my family, starting a new business ... and *catching up on a lot of sleep!*

Do I regret those eight "challenging" months at CBS News? Not a chance.

I learned a helluva lot. *I learned you can't be something you're not. I learned some things just won't change no matter what you do. I learned you have to get out when it's wrong for you or you will make yourself sick. I learned that timing is everything. I learned you can't deplete your energy. And I learned that the support of friends and family will see you through anything.*

∾

The personal challenges I faced during that one year seemed overwhelming to me at the time, but they were small in comparison to what my friend Irv Cross has experienced over and over in seeking success as a black man in a predominantly white society. Irv credits many of the same lessons I learned with keeping him going. He is a master of the art of rising above whatever challenges he has faced.

Irv was one of my coanchors (with Brent Musberger) on *The NFL Today*. He brought something special to our team because he was a former player—a cornerback and, for a time, player/defensive backfield coach with the Philadelphia Eagles, recognized during his playing years as one of the best tacklers among defensive backs in the NFL. Irv was a man of many and varied accomplishments off the field as well as on, including a stint as a retail stockbroker on Wall Street, and his subsequent positions as athletic director at the college-university level seem to me a perfect place for him. I'm so pleased that young people are now able to benefit from the combination of his athletic experience and his leadership ability.

Over the ten years we worked together, I came to value Irv not only for his expertise but for his on-air commentary and the fact that he was just the nicest person in the world to work with. So I was stunned to learn later that when he joined CBS Sports in 1971, Irv had to stand up for himself and not be forced to fit into someone else's caricature of what he should be.

"I wanted to do a good job," Irv remembers, "and I wanted to make a positive statement with my appearance. I saw myself as a leader and symbol on that show to project an image of a former player who had become a professional broadcaster. But I soon realized they wanted me to project an image of some 'Superfly' type. Before we went on the air, I was taken down to Barney's men's store on the West Side. The wardrobe people had me put on a light blue leisure suit with dark blue stripes around the collar. They added a blue and white flowered silk shirt unbuttoned to show the four hairs on my chest and a gold medallion necklace."

Irv was shocked. "That's what they wanted me to wear on air? I couldn't do it. It wasn't me. I always worked with a coat and tie on when I worked on Wall Street. I would never have worn something like that 'Superfly' outfit."

He decided to take a stand. "I called up the producer and said, 'Look, I don't dress that way. It's not my personality.' It wasn't an easy thing for me to do. I figured it meant I would be taken off the show. I really thought that phone call was it. But I knew I had to make the decision to let people know how I felt about it. Well, the producer, Bob Wussler, thought about it for a couple of days. Then he called me up. 'Dress the way you want,' he said. 'Wear what you want.' So I came in with a coat and tie, and that was how I always appeared on the air."

Of course, that form of racism was subtle in comparison to what Irv had faced earlier in his life. He grew up in the 1960s in Hammond, Indiana, a town with 60,000 people but only a few black families. As a result, he had mostly white friends in school. Not everyone in the town was friendly, however. People would occasionally yell racial slurs at him whether he was alone or with his white friends. Irv was a hotshot athlete in high school, and he remembers one time going to a restaurant across the street from school with his friends, but the restaurant refused to let him come in. "We don't serve Negroes," they said. Irv's friends rallied around him and said if the restaurant wouldn't serve him, they wouldn't go either.

Many years later when Irv was a well-known athlete with the Eagles, he and his wife bought a piece of land in Philadelphia to build a house on. But to his surprise, after he bought it, some people filed an injunction to keep them out of the area. "The man who sold the land to us said, 'I don't dislike you personally. As a matter of fact I'm a big Eagles fan. But I didn't mean to sell that land to you, and I'm going to have to cancel our agreement.' So here was a person who would buy a ticket to the games and cheer me on wildly, but he didn't want to live next door to me," Irv recalls.

Irv felt a combination of anger and hurt. Still, he was able to separate himself from the situation. "I knew that people make judgments based on their experiences that had nothing to do with me. I've always felt, every day, that these were opportunities to learn. I didn't feel bitterness. I just tried to understand what was going on."

Now Irv is athletic director at Macalester College, a private liberal arts college in St. Paul, Minnesota, where he imparts the lessons he has learned to young people. "The reason I took this job," he says, "was because I believe the athletic experience, no matter what level you play, little league to professional, is very important in helping to develop one's personality and strength. You learn how it feels to win and to lose, and most importantly, you learn how to come back from a loss. It was like those racial slurs. I would fall down, but I knew I could come back up. *It's what you learn to do when you lose that is most important. You have to learn to accept the loss and say to yourself, 'Okay, on this day, they were better than me. But how can I be better next time?' I learned that when negative things happen, I can't do anything about it then. But I can focus on trying to make the world a better place than it was yesterday.*"

~

Everyone has good and bad days, good and bad years. Walter, Johnny, Irv, and I have had our fair share of both.

We've learned that life isn't perfect, but that you can get past the "imperfect" times if you accept who you are and appreciate what you have. Count your blessings, and know that what is bad today is better tomorrow. Remember that a pessimist sees difficulty in every opportunity; an optimist sees opportunity in every difficulty. Be an optimist.

Lesson

9

KEEP YOUR PERSPECTIVE

Years ago, I would worry about the most ridiculous things, replaying them over and over in my mind. Why did I say that? Why did I do that? I can't believe she said that to me; what did she mean? Did he really say that? Should I have responded differently? Now, however, I've learned to be a big picture person.

It's all about perspective. You know what it's like when you're in a difficult situation and someone says to you, "Don't let it get you down! You just have to keep your perspective on things." Okay—but what exactly does that really mean? The answer came to me when I hiked to the top of a mountain range outside of Tucson, Arizona. There, high above the trees, roads, and houses, I could see for miles and miles in the distance. The panoramic view was awe-inspiring, reminding me that whatever concerns I had at the time were truly minuscule—so tiny, so insignificant.

That experience gave me a visual image for what it means to "have perspective" on something. So now, when someone has done something hurtful to you or you've had a setback or made a mistake, recall my mountaintop story. It will help you put those incidents in context. This technique also boosts your confidence because it enables you to take control of the situation. *If you can't change your situation, change your outlook.*

I learned this lesson when working with Jimmy "the Greek" Snyder, one of my colleagues at *The NFL Today*. A big raucous man who would never in his life win any etiquette contests, Jimmy was a Vegas oddsmaker who became a football prognosticator and analyst on our show. Although he was an entertaining and at times colorful character, Jimmy was a dichotomy: He seemed to have two sides to him.

There were times when you could sit down and have a perfectly pleasant conversation with him. But at other times he could be downright hurtful. He seemed to have real problems with the fact that a woman was at the sports desk, and I felt that he was seizing every opportunity to throw me off balance. We'd be going on live in twenty seconds, and he'd start making inappropriate comments with sexual overtones to see how I would react. He was playing mind games with me.

This happened repeatedly over a period of time. At first I tried to laugh it off, thinking, Oh, that's just Jimmy. Then I tried to ignore him. But it really did bother me. To him, it was teasing; to me, it was a constant barrage of tension-inducing moments. After all, this was happening minutes, sometimes even seconds, prior to going live! Finally, I refused to ignore it anymore when I read an interview he gave to *People* magazine. "Oh, yeah, she's a gorgeous kid," he said, "but you have to prop her up with a cue card. And of course, all the guys think bad thoughts when they look at her."

Well, that was it for me: I'd had it with such expressions of bad taste. I was out there working my buns off, trying to be successful as a woman sportscaster, and he was dragging women back to the Dark Ages with his sexist remarks. The show was very popular, the ratings were great, and I loved my job. I'm strong and can handle pressure, but I have limits to what I'll put up with and wasn't going to accept this anymore.

It was a big step for me when I marched into the producer's office and told him "Either he goes or I do." He tried to calm me down, saying we were all part of one big family. Yeah, a dysfunctional family, I thought to myself. Families don't always get along, he said, but still we are family.

My lawyer at the time, the powerful Ed Hookstratten, called CBS management and told them that unless they made changes, I was out of there. Jimmy's behavior was clearly harassment, although we didn't call it that at the time. So Mike Pearl, our wonderful and creative executive producer, came up with a solution. Jimmy would come to the studio early on Sundays to tape his segments, and after he left, my cohosts Brent Musberger and Irv Cross, and I would arrive on the set to do the pregame show live. The director would play back Jimmy's segment during the half-hour broadcast.

This solution worked for a year until I returned from maternity leave after my daughter's birth. While I was away, Jimmy had returned to the set for live portions of the pregame show, and he sat in my chair next to Brent. He'd become quite comfortable in my seat, plus he had gotten more air time while I was gone. Jimmy's on-set position was moved to the end of the anchor desk, standing next to my chair farther away from Brent. Immediately I could feel the tension on the set. It was clear Jimmy was fuming at Brent for some reason.

That night at an East Side bar called Peartrees, as I read in the paper Monday morning, Jimmy challenged Brent, saying he paid more attention to me than to Jimmy on the air that Sunday. Brent *had* talked to me more that day since it was my first day back on set after my daughter's birth, but he was merely welcoming me back home. So when Jimmy accused Brent of ignoring him, Brent asked him what he was talking about. Suddenly Jimmy wound up and punched Brent, knocking him to the floor. The next day the front page of the *New York Daily News* had my picture, full page, and the heading "The Face That Launched the Barroom Brawl." I was shocked and hoped my mother would never see it—she just wouldn't understand.

This incident, however, was a turning point in my attitude toward Jimmy. I knew that one of his children had died from cystic fibrosis and that a second child was also very ill with the disease. Having children of my own, I wondered how anyone could survive losing a child. I wondered if a lot of his anger and frustration had stemmed from being away from home so much and not being able to face his children's illness. I actually felt sorry for this man who was so unhappy that he would sock a coworker in the jaw. I didn't want to be upset with him anymore. This experience taught me something about dealing with difficult people: ***Don't carry a grudge. It will eat away at you over time. You must put things in context by understanding the other person's point of view.***

Back at the studio the following Sunday we all made a pact to deal with the very public brawl between Jimmy and Brent with humor. We knew we had to take another approach with Jimmy and accept that he was just ... different.

That day, I finished my interview piece, then I tossed it to Brent and Jimmy, who stood on either side of the big board behind me to talk about the games for the day.

"And now ... let's go over to Brent and Jimmy," I began. From underneath the desk I pulled out a musical triangle: We were using it as a small version of the big ones used in the old-time boxing matches. I clanged it with a little wand. *"Round two!"*

Cut to Brent and Jimmy. When Brent raised his pointer to the game board, he was wearing a red boxing glove. Everybody laughed. It eased the tension and changed the situation into something we could manage.

Jimmy died in 1996, and I'm sad he's not with us anymore. In a funny sort of way, I miss him. After what he'd said about me in *People*, it's ironic that the same magazine asked me to write something when he passed away. I wrote a page, but what they used was this: "You either loved him or you loved to hate him." I guess that said it all.

In the end I learned to accept Jimmy as he was. He wasn't going to change. Or if he did change, it wouldn't be because of me. Remember: ***It's not about you; it's about them. Refuse to let others' problems become your problem. They own it; you don't. Changing people and helping them solve their problems is the job of trained professionals. Change how you deal with the relationship rather than trying to change the person. That's one way to keep your perspective.***

∽

When my friend Coach Rick Pitino was brought in to turn a small basketball program around, he also had to distinguish what he could change from what he couldn't in his search for success. Now the head coach at the University of Louisville, Rick is known as one of the premier coaches in basketball. Of course, I especially enjoyed his taking the University of Kentucky Wildcats to a national championship. Off the court, he is a tremendous motivational speaker, and he was one of the first coaches to write books about applying the techniques he'd developed in sports to a winning attitude in business. The books, *Suceess Is a Choice* and *Lead to Succeed*, are best-sellers.

Back in 1986 Rick was an assistant coach for the New York Knicks under Hubie Brown and feeling good about being part of the team's success at the professional level. But the university level came calling when Providence College in Rhode Island offered him a head coaching job. Rick was intrigued, but after seeing the team play in the Big East tournament, he decided the job of making them competitive was nearly impossible. The team had three good players who were graduating and not another single player whose average was in double digits. Plus the school had little capability of attracting good high school players. He agreed to have dinner with the athletic director to turn the job down in person.

At the dinner the athletic director admitted how pathetic the team had been. However, he said they were committed to changing it entirely and were confident that Pitino could do it. "He was emphatic," Rick says, "leaving no doubt that I was to take the job." As a result, Rick started to feel totally challenged and motivated by the job. To his own surprise, by the end of the dinner he'd accepted.

When he arrived at Providence and saw the players, his heart sank. "It was everything I thought it would be, only worse," he says. "The players were all overweight and out of shape and had no basketball skills."

In fact, they seemed so unprepared and so untalented that his first thought for how to fix the situation was simply to get rid of them! That way he could bring in other, more promising players as replacements. "The starting center was a defector from Poland," says Pitino, "and after watching him play, I wanted to notify the Polish authorities of his whereabouts. He was that bad." The other guard was a transfer from the Indiana program who had been a high school phenomenon but couldn't make it at IU. His self-confidence was shattered.

Billy Donovan, another young player, Pitino recalls, "came in like the Pillsbury Dough-Boy, 5 feet, 11 inches, 191 pounds. He wanted to transfer, and I wanted him to transfer so I could have the scholarship." But both programs he wanted rejected him. "When he came back in to see me," Rick says, "I said, 'Look, Billy, why don't you stick this out? You can come in as the fourth guard in the program. With our running offense, you'll get some playing time. You'll get a good education and have some good times and be part of the team. But if you agree to this, here's what I want you to do.'" Rick gave him a workout program for the summer. He told Donovan to come back thirty pounds lighter; plus he had to learn to make a jump shot.

Rick had discovered that he couldn't ditch the entire team and start over. He couldn't change the situation, so he had to change his perspective. He had to take what he had, try to fix some elements, and see what would happen. The changes he wanted were not minor corrections for the players to make, yet he was able to motivate them by showing them the big picture—what they would gain if they did what he asked. He didn't get bogged down worrying about what he didn't have and what he couldn't fix; he set to work to improve what he had.

To his surprise, the players came back in the fall ready to play. All had made dramatic progress. Donovan had lost thirty pounds, and the Polish center had given up smoking. Then Pitino had to teach them the skills they needed. "The first thing I did was make every player earn and deserve self-esteem by getting them in the best shape of their lives," he says. "What I had to do was put them on an improvement regimen. Back then there were no restrictions on the number of hours we could practice. So we'd practice before breakfast, between classes, at regular practice time after dinner, and again late at night."

"And before my eyes was transformed a team that I'd called the 'Bad News Bears' in dead last place to a team that was competitive," Rick remembers. "Billy Donovan had gone from the Pillsbury Dough-Boy to the name I still use for him, Billy the Kid. He literally dominated college basketball. Every single player took his game to a new level."

Soon the progress was evident in the team's wins. That first year, they lost seven games at the buzzer and went to the NCAA tournament for the first time in ten years. The second year they won seven games at the buzzer and again went to the tournament. In the Elite Eight they played Georgetown, which had beaten Providence badly the two times the schools had met that year. But in the postseason, when it counted most, Providence won.

"This team that had no self-esteem and no talent," says Rick, "had developed a work ethic second to none and ended up going to every college basketball player's dream: the Final Four. It was a true Cinderella story." Billy Donovan is now the highly regarded head coach of men's basketball at the University of Florida.

When Pitino had been approached about the job, people had told him not to take it. They said a coach at a small New England school in the highly competitive Big East Conference would never be able to recruit good players. For them, that meant he would never be able to have a winnng team. But Rick had not tried to fix what couldn't be fixed. Instead he accepted what was given to him, worked hard at changing what he *could* change, and had success as a result.

~

Like Rick Pitino, my dear friend, the multitalented Kathie Lee Gifford, one of America's favorite TV personalities, also has an amazing ability to keep her perspective by staying focused on her passions. Even after what she calls a "lifetime of being told 'I couldn't … I shouldn't … and I definitely wouldn't,'" she has constantly moved toward what she loves and refuses to let others define her.

Music was the first love in Kathie's life. Yet, after a young Kathie sang for a few minutes in an appointment with a voice teacher, the teacher smiled and said, "Honey, stick to harmony." It wasn't easy news to hear. "It hurts to be told you're not very good at something," Kathie says, "but in this case, I let that hurt motivate me into *doing* something about it. I studied, I practiced, I performed every chance I got and I grew better because of it."

Thirty-six years later, she's still committed to constant improvement. Kathie has continued to study voice, and has just started recording her twentieth CD. She's performed the National Anthem at the Super Bowl, sung with symphonies, at Carnegie Hall, in Las Vegas, Atlantic City, and on TV specials and Broadway.

Kathie admits that, by keeping her perspective, she has enjoyed a lifetime involving her passion. She reminds us to not let "the opinions of others define who you are."

~

Just as some situations can be fixed and others can't, there are some mistakes you can correct and others you can't. Everybody makes mistakes. But when you're working on live television, your mistake is out there for the world to see—and see again and again. Considering what's said and done on television today, the faux pas I made on the *CBS Morning News* in 1985 seems small. But at that time, in that context, it was big enough to generate a torrent of criticism from the media and the public. Johnny Carson even made a joke in a monologue on the *Tonight Show*. It took me a long time to get over what nearly everybody, including myself, thought was a Texas-size mistake. In fact, the entire episode was so dispiriting that I didn't talk about it with anyone then.

It was my fifth month in my new job as coanchor of the show, and I had just returned from a ten-day trip to London covering the fortieth anniversary of the end of World War II in Europe—VE Day. Unlike the other networks' morning shows (*Today* and *Good Morning America*), ours was still defined as a hard news program. Still (as I explained in Chapter 8), I'd been brought over from my long-running success cohosting *The NFL Today* to enliven the coverage and try to raise the show's dismal ratings. It had been in third place for thirty years. I thought the transition would be easier than it was. But after this particular week, we'd gotten encouragement about our coverage from London, and things seemed to be moving in the right direction.

After the trans-Atlantic flight back to New York, I was wiped out—jet-lagged, sleep-deprived, and exhausted. With very little time to rest, we returned bright and early Monday morning. Some people need more sleep than others, and I need a lot!

As a result, it felt like I was sleepwalking through that morning's newscast. I just wanted it to be over so I could go home and get some rest. But at the commercial break in the last hour, our producer ran up to me. With great excitement, he announced "they" were here and I had to interview "the couple."

"What couple?" I asked.

The story was about a woman who had accused a man of raping and kidnapping her and then recanted her accusation after he'd served six years in prison. The judge wasn't convinced by the woman's change of testimony and denied the motion for a new trial, but with so many questions about the conviction, the governor commuted the man's sentence to time already served and released him.

Of course, I knew about the story, but not all the details. The buzz around the set was that the man and the woman were going around the city together in a limo with a publicist, generating publicity that could help them get a book or movie deal. *We* knew they were going to be on the *Today Show* and *Good Morning America*, and our producers had left messages for them but had gotten no response. Now, however, they'd just shown up unannounced.

Everyone was rushing around the studio, and the producer said he was going to have them miked so we could do the interview! I suggested Bill Kurtis do it—but the producer insisted that I do the interview. He gave me a quick recap of the story: bottom line, the woman said the man raped her, he went to jail, she recanted her testimony, he was released, and now she's sorry. I knew that much already and told him I needed more information than that! But there wasn't time for more. There wasn't even time for me to pull my thoughts together. One minute later, the man, the woman, and I were sitting before the cameras ready to go live. As best I can remember, I first said that it must have been a rather difficult time for them.

They both nodded, smiling sheepishly. I made a few more state-ments about how rough it must be for them and asked a cou-ple of questions. They responded and kept nodding.

Since my impression was that they had made up, I looked directly at the man and said, "How about a hug?"

Oh, God. Did I say that? It popped out of my mouth on live television! I wasn't being flippant; I do believe in forgiveness. But who did I think I was trying to bring these two people together, especially on a news show? Yes, my defenses were down, but it just slipped out. In the awkward pause that fol-lowed, I knew instantly it was inappropriate and I wished I could shove those words back into my mouth.

There was a moment's pause on the set. The man and woman moved toward each other, shoulders touching ... and then stopped.

Had they hugged, this evidence of their reconciliation would have made headlines. But they didn't. After the segment ended, the producer came out of the control room and told me I'd done a good job.

But when I went home that day, I felt in my gut that I hadn't done my best. I was frustrated that I was forced to do an interview I wasn't prepared for and hadn't researched. Nothing felt right.

I also wasn't prepared for what happened the next morn-ing, when I got blasted in the newspapers and on TV and radio shows all around the country. At the time, such personal ques-tions were not being asked on TV, and if they were, it would certainly not happen on news shows. There was still a clear line drawn between news and entertainment, especially at CBS, and I had crossed it. I later learned from a colleague that one of the top bananas at our show was calling the media him-self and saying, "Did you see what Phyllis did?" I had not been his choice to cohost the show in the first place, and now I'd given him ammunition to attack me. Because I came from the sports and entertainment world and wasn't considered a "hard news" journalist, everything I said or did was magnified.

I realize now I could have deflected some of the criticism if I had talked about it openly. But I thought that if I tried to explain it, it would create more problems.

My one supporter in the media at that time was a *New York Times* reporter who told me privately that if they had hugged, it would have made big news. He praised me for having the guts to ask them to show that they'd forgiven each other. A more seasoned broadcaster could have gotten away with it, he said, but because you're the new kid on the block, it was too risky.

I kept showing up each morning, smiling, trying to do my job, hoping that the criticism would die down and go away. At least that was what I did in public. In private I was being tough on myself, asking: Was it really *that* bad? Should I respond to the critics? Should I just ignore it? In the middle of the night I would replay the interview in my head. It was like the quarterback on a football team who has lost an important game and keeps reviewing the plays over and over to try and figure out how he could have done it differently. Why didn't that play work? If only I'd called a running play instead of passing the ball …

Finally, my friend, the columnist Liz Smith helped shake me out of this nightmare with a handwritten note that said, "Just shrug it off and say, 'Well, I won't do that again,' or 'I did what I thought was best' or 'Hell, that was awful!'—and then forge ahead! Just as many people loved what you did as didn't. You have excellent impulses! Forget all that other bull—!"

She was right. What was I getting so worked up for? This was a minor judgment error on my part on a TV show. ***This was not the end of the world. Life goes on.***

Later I heard that the other morning show hosts had asked the man and woman more personal questions as well. On *Good Morning America*, the cohost had asked: "What were the first things you said to each other?" And on *Today*, the coanchor had asked: "Who would you like to see play you in the movie?" On reflection, I see that a big part of my problem in handling that incident was that I wasted an enormous amount of time and energy wishing it hadn't happened! I was trying to fix something that couldn't be fixed.

I learned from this incident: *If you can't take it back, take it forward. When you say something you shouldn't have, it's impossible to take it back, no matter how much you wish you could. Release it. If apologizing will help, do it. If promising never to do it again will help, do it. Then you must move on. Remember that the incident is one moment in a lifetime of experiences. Think about what really matters: your loved ones, your health, your accomplishments. That's how you put the incident in perspective and get beyond it. Use it to grow so you don't get into that kind of situation again.*

John, my husband at the time, was incredibly supportive of me. In fact, he has turned the incident into a running joke. At last year's Kentucky Derby when I ran into him, the first thing he said was, "Hi, Phyl … how 'bout a hug!" We had a good laugh.

∽

We all make mistakes, have to deal with challenging colleagues, and face situations we're trying to turn around. At times it's so overwhelming that you have no perspective on the situation at all. The little agonies seem monumental, and the things that are really important in life get pushed aside as if they were merely the minutiae. It's not just that you can't see the forest for the trees; you're stuck down there covered with leaves! Here's what to do. Rise above it. Rise so far above it that you feel 10,000 feet off the ground. Then you will have the perspective you need to sort it all out. You will see what really matters in life and what is unimportant in the grand scheme of things.

10

LEARN TO LAUGH AT YOURSELF

After many years of taking the mishaps of life way too seriously, I think I've finally mastered the healthy art of laughing at myself. It's one of the lessons that Dr. Norman Vincent Peale taught me: We must learn to look on life in humorous ways. It seems that I've had plenty of opportunities to perfect this lesson. I've called people the wrong name on camera. I've wished I could shove words back into my mouth as soon as I said them or shove food out of my mouth as soon as I ate it. But sometimes you have to make a joke and move on.

Take my experience working on the box office hit *Meet the Parents*. Although I'd studied acting with the well-known teachers Warren Robertson and Darryl Hickman when I first moved to New York, I'd never been in a movie before—though many thought I had. To get my role I auditioned, along with several other women, for director Jay Roach of *Austin Powers* fame. His parents grew up in the panhandle of Texas, so when he heard my Texas accent, it sounded very familiar to him, like family. I'm convinced it helped me get the part.

The film stars one of the cinema's greatest actors—Robert De Niro. In awe and a bit intimidated, I hung back a bit from the cast for the first few days. But soon I felt comfortable and started asking all sorts of questions.

On one of my more curious days, De Niro looked over and threw me one of his eyebrows-up, *Taxi Driver* looks.

"Phyllis," he asked, eyes fixed on me. "Is this your first movie?"

I gave *him* my best "you-talkin'-to-me?" look.

"Yes," I admitted, "it is."

"I thought so," and he flashed his wonderful, crinkly-eyed smile.

Uh-oh. What did *that* mean?

In case you're trying to place me, I played the small role of Linda Banks, whose son, "Dr. Bob," is marrying De Niro's younger daughter. Though I was in over twenty scenes, I had only a few lines. Remember when Ben Stiller overslept and stumbled into the kitchen in his pajamas with his hair sticking up to discover both families sitting there over breakfast? I was the one who said, "Oh, looks like someone had a little visit from the hair fairy!"

On another day we were filming a scene set in the living room, where the two families in the movie had gathered to discuss the wedding schedule. My job was to sit on the couch, nod, smile, and fake some vague background conversation.

Well, I don't know what happened to me that day. It was either nervous energy or too much coffee. Or maybe it was just the real Phyllis aching to do a stellar job and shine in my little part. But as soon as the cameras started to roll, I began jabbering away as if I were hosting a party in my own home.

"*Cutttt!*" yelled Jay Roach, and we all looked up, startled.

"Uh, Phyllis, you don't need to talk so much in this scene. *You don't actually have any lines here.*"

My face went crimson. I was in the middle of the entire cast, sitting next to these great actors—Bob (he likes to be called Bob), Ben, Blythe Danner, and others—and there I was, looking like I was trying to steal the scene. I wanted to slide underneath the couch and disappear.

But one of the most helpful lessons I've learned (and use daily) is to not take everything so seriously. Instead of being embarrassed, I tried to view my blunder with more humor and less judgment. Was it really that big of a deal? No. It was my first movie, and I was bound to make some mistakes. Did I really cause a big problem? No. It was just one more clip for the cutting room floor. So instead of cowering and being hard on myself, as I usually am, I made a joke of it.

"I'm so sorry, everyone," I said to the group. "I didn't mean to talk so much. It's just … I felt so at home. I thought I was in my own living room!"

Everyone laughed, and it was forgotten instantly. They blew it off right away. And the scene ended up being cut anyway.

~

My ability to laugh at myself also helped me through another awkward moment with a movie star a few years ago, when I co-chaired the American Cancer Society's "Mother of the Year" luncheon honoring Kathie Lee Gifford. First Lady of the State of New York Libby Pataki was the honorary chair, and Regis Philbin, Rosie O'Donnell, Joan Rivers, and many others also attended. But I wanted one more person whose presence would make it extra-special for Kathie. My assistant Dee suggested Kevin Costner. Great idea, I thought. Kevin and his children had been frequent houseguests at Frank and Kathie's home. But I thought he was probably off promoting his latest movie at that time, *Message in a Bottle*, and would not be available.

In fact, the idea made me a little nervous because, like many women, I had had a not-so-secret crush on Kevin for years. I'll admit it here: I saw *Dances with Wolves* five times!

Despite my nervousness, I knew he would be a fun surprise for Kathie, and I remembered another of my mottos: if you don't ask, you don't get. So I wrote a letter, suggesting he surprise Kathie at the luncheon and Fed-Ex'ed it with the invitation to his office in California. I knew because of his schedule it was a long shot. A few days later, though, I was thrilled when his office called to say he'd love to attend! Plus, he liked the idea of being an unannounced guest.

By the day of the luncheon in the ballroom at the St. Regis Hotel, I had calmed my nerves, especially when I saw how excited Kathie, her family, and the other guests were when they arrived and discovered he was there. The room was still buzzing when we sat down for lunch. I had seated Kevin next to me, and I found him to be very easy to talk with. He was so nice, and even more charming and handsome in person than he was on the big screen. We chatted easily between bites of poached salmon and sautéed spinach. Before I knew it, I was being introduced to speak.

Suddenly, Kevin leaned toward me to say something in my ear, and I went silent, my heart skipping a beat.

"Phyllis," he whispered, *"you have a big, green thing in your teeth."*

My mouth must have fallen open, before I quickly squeezed my lips together. The spinach, I thought. I put my hand over my mouth as I tried to use my tongue to get rid of it. I looked at Kevin again, with a kind of fake smile, teeth together, for him to check my teeth again, praying that it was gone.

"No, no ... it's right *there*," he instructed, pointing to the identical spot on his own teeth.

I tried again, using my finger this time.

"No! To the right ... to the *right*!"

Finally, I took a sip of water and swished it around. Then I opened my mouth and smiled.

"It's okay now," he whispered, patting me on the shoulder, "it's gone," just at the moment the emcee said, "Ladies and gentlemen, please welcome Phyllis George."

As I made my way to the podium, I looked over at Kevin. He had a smile on his face, and I had to chuckle as well. I had survived a most embarrassing moment with America's heart-throb, and if I was feeling a little less dignified, I also felt relief that he seemed to be sharing the moment with me.

Kevin gave a wonderful impromptu speech about Kathie Lee. I haven't seen him since then, but he certainly endeared himself to me forever that day. Many people would avoid calling attention to something that was awkward or embarrassing. But he did, and I was extremely grateful. Even a larger-than-life movie idol knows that life is full of awkward, human moments and you just have to laugh at them.

Laughter is your secret survival weapon. It has pulled me through some of the most embarrassing and awkward moments of my life. Don't be so hard on yourself. Describe your "moment" as if it were a scene in a sitcom. Then you'll see it's usually not as bad as you think.

~

My first attempt using the humor approach was during the Miss America pageant, when I dropped my crown on live television. It happened as I walked down the famous runway at the Convention Hall in Atlantic City as Bert Parks crooned, "There she is ..."

As I nodded to the judges to say thank you, the crown slipped off my head, came tumbling down, and hit the runway. Stones popped out and scattered everywhere. This was a "first." In the entire history of the Miss America pageant, I was the first (and *only*, thank you very much) to drop her crown. What do I do? I paused for a moment, then bent down and picked it up as my robe drooped to my elbows. So with the scepter in one hand and the crown in the other, I continued my walk with hands full, robe falling, and hair sticking up on top where the crown had fallen off. It was not the end of the world, but it *was* my big moment on national TV in front of 30 million viewers. What a picture!

A day later I was already thinking: How can I turn this into something positive? My opportunity came two nights later. I had been invited to be a guest on the *Tonight Show* and was looking forward to meeting Johnny Carson, the king of late-night TV. I knew Carson had once said that talking to a Miss America is like talking to a redwood fence. They have pat answers and aren't spontaneous, he'd said: they just sit there with their hands neatly folded on their laps and their ankles crossed at a perfect angle. I was nervous, but I was a fan of Carson and was determined to impress him. Unlike the other

Miss Americas, most of whom had worn their gowns and crowns on the show, I showed up in a cocktail dress and crown-less.

"Well, Phyllis … our new Miss America! How are you?" Johnny said, greeting me. "Why aren't you wearing your crown? *Are you afraid you'll drop it?*"

Everyone laughed. Very funny, I thought. He'd started poking fun at me right away. So I just smiled and said, "That's right, Johnny. I'm the klutzy Miss America. *But I bet you'll never forget me.*"

Johnny and the audience loved it! What was this? A Miss America who can laugh at herself? Everyone took my cue that it was okay to laugh at my crown-dropping incident. And I mean *everyone*. When I met John Wayne at a Neiman Marcus charity event a few months later, my chaperone (can you believe I ever had a chaperone?!) immediately blurted out to him: "Oh, Mr. Wayne, Phyllis does a great impersonation of you!"

He looked at me quizzically and asked, "Well, why dontcha show it to me, missy?"

I thought to myself, You're *not* going to do this. But I did. I put my hands on my hips, swaggered a few steps (as if I had a very heavy gun in my holster), turned around, cocked my head, and said in my best John Wayne voice: "We were lookin' for 'em yesss-ter-day and here they are tuh-day. Now-let's-go-gettum…."

The Duke laughed. And then he one-upped me.

"I'd do my impersonation of *you*, lit-tle la-dy," he smiled, "but-I-don't have a crown ta drop!" Ha! Ha! Ha!

At the end of my reign, the crown incident was immortalized in a poem for the official Miss America program booklet. Next to a big photo of me holding my crown, it read:

She's the first Miss America to lose her crown!
As she stepped on the runway it came tumbling down!
Scarcely missing a step, composure so grand,
She continued her walk—with crown in hand!

~

My beautiful and successful friend Paula Zahn, an Emmy-winning broadcaster, is one of the most clever people I know. A twenty-three-year news veteran with a remarkable career at CBS, ABC, and Fox, Paula is now earning rave reviews as anchor for CNN's flagship morning news program, *American Morning with Paula Zahn*. Earlier in her career, Paula used her sense of humor to nail an important news assignment.

She was in Cuba, eight months pregnant and covering President Fidel Castro's summit meeting with Mikhail Gorbachev for ABC News at the time. It was her first foreign assignment on her first network job, and she wasn't going to let her burgeoning body interfere with this coup ... or so she thought. Little did she know it would be her best asset.

"Even though those of us covering the summit had been told no one would get an interview with Castro," she recalls, "I certainly was going to land one." Her producer thought she was crazy. The network was so worried she would go into labor in Cuba, they had a corporate jet on standby to fly her to Miami if necessary.

At the news conference at the end of the summit, Paula says, "I jostled my way through the crowd of journalists to the ABC News platform, where I could barely squeeze in. The news conference started—and went on for several hours. President Castro's bodyguards became so concerned about 'my condition' in the hot, overcrowded room that they kept handing me bottles of water and crackers."

Her new bodyguard friends then warned her that Castro's exit was going to be frenzied when the news conference ended, and they led her to the door Castro would use so she wouldn't be trampled in the rush. She was in the perfect position to stop Castro as he left, but what would she use as her tactic? What intriguing question could she ask that would make him pause? With a belly out to *there*, she must have thought it was time to put this big baby-to-be to work. She waddled to the center of the doorway.

"As Castro walked past," Paula says, "I stepped forward with my enormous belly blocking his path, and I asked him a question in Spanish. And there we stood, belly to belly."

It was an absurd sight, to be sure. Enough to make some of the reporters in the room grin. There was just no way he could get past her tummy. Paula smiled at Castro and held her microphone up, waiting for her interview.

"He stopped, looked down at me—amused or amazed, I don't know which—and began talking," she says, "and I walked away that day with my first exclusive interview with a world leader for ABC News."

"Say what you will about Castro," Paula adds, "but in that instance he was a true gentleman. I still think of it as a triumph of guts *and* girth."

Paula had turned a tense moment into a winning opportunity. Humor takes the edge off. It brings out the best—and most humane—qualities in all of us.

~

Embarrassing things happen. What are you going to do ... hide? You'll make yourself and those around you more comfortable if you hold your head up and laugh with the rest of them. I tell myself this bit of advice over and over because somehow I'm always getting myself into these predicaments.

Over two decades ago, while visiting President and Mrs. Carter at the White House, I had a fashion emergency of epic proportions. It was not long after John had become governor of Kentucky, and President Jimmy Carter had invited us to a black-tie dinner. Our schedule was so busy that we packed for the trip in a hurry. We raced to catch the flight that would take us to Washington, dressed in our formal wear to go straight to the event.

When we got there, a member of the White House staff took our bags up to the Lincoln bedroom, where we would stay overnight, and unpacked for us as we made our way to the pre-dinner reception. *Now this was service!*

But soon I discovered I had a problem. I was pregnant and just beginning to show, and my evening gown was not fitting me right. I felt really uncomfortable, fearing I'd made the wrong choice for what to wear and it was too late to do anything about it.

Then, my discomfort became even worse. As I moved forward in the reception line to shake President and Mrs. Carter's hands, a large man behind me stepped on the train of my gown. *RIIIIP!* Oh, no!

Now my dress was ripped at the waist and had a huge hole in the back. Since I was only one person away from the president by then, I couldn't step out of line, so I gamely proceeded along, hoping no one would notice. But after greeting him and Mrs. Carter, I had to do something to hold my gown together for the rest of the evening since I had nothing else to wear. As I looked around the room, my eyes fell on the Marine guards, and instantly the phrase "send in the Marines" took on a whole new meaning! When I asked one of them for help, he motioned to a staff member and asked her to bring some safety pins. Then, the Marines stood guard around me in a corner of one of the halls away from the crowd while she frantically pinned my gown together. Believe me: it looked bad! *Women's Wear Daily* agreed, dubbing me a "fashion victim." I'd been called a lot of things, but this was a new one!

Too bad the magazine's correspondent wasn't there to catch my outfit the next day because my fashion nightmare wasn't over. The next morning when we got up, we weren't sure of the protocol. Do we go downstairs? Does someone bring us breakfast? There were no instructions on the desk—just a phone and a framed copy of the Gettysburg Address.

I picked up the phone to check with the White House operator. "Yes, Mrs. Brown," she said politely. "Mrs. Carter is waiting for you in the family dining room."

We made a mad dash to get ready. Shower, shave, get dressed ... *get dressed* ... where were my clothes? My red turtleneck sweater and my black suede boots were there in the closet, but no black skirt. In my haste, I had forgotten to pack it! How could I have done this? Me? My choices for breakfast were my torn ball gown, my black ranch mink coat (we all wore them then), and my nightgown and matching robe. Which would you choose? ***Lesson: Always pack more than you need. You never know when you may have an emergency and need another option.***

I put on my robe—it was a beautiful embroidered one from my wedding trousseau—and hoped for the best. But when I walked into the breakfast room, everyone else was dressed. We all made polite chitchat, everyone trying hard not to notice what I was wearing. Finally, I was so embarrassed that somewhere between the eggs and the toast, I had to come clean.

"I just have to tell you all," I began, "I'm really, really embarrassed. We were so excited about coming here and sleeping in the Lincoln bedroom that I forgot to pack my skirt!"

Everybody laughed, and I began to feel a little better. The First Lady graciously began to assure me that we would work something out when her mother-in-law, the famous Miss Lillian, interrupted. "Now, you come with me, honey," she said, taking me by the hand. "I've got something nice you can wear. Don't you worry: I'll take care of it." She led me to the room across the hall from the Lincoln bedroom. It was the Queen's bedroom, where she was staying. She reached into her closet and pulled out a pair of size fourteen, polyester, elastic-waist, golf-green stretch pants.

"Here, dear. Put these on. Then you can just wear them home."

What could I do? This was the president's mother—you do what she says. I wasn't about to ask her if I could pick out something else.

I went back to our room, put on the pants, rolled them up at the waist, and tucked the legs into my boots. Then I stayed in the room chatting with Miss Lillian the rest of the morning while John was in meetings. At least, I thought, the president wasn't going to see me like this.

Then at 3 p.m., John and I were in the room getting ready to leave when the phone rang. "The president would like you to stop by the Oval Office on your way out for a little visit," said one of his assistants.

"John, I can't!" I was frantic.

"Just put your mink coat over them, and he'll never notice."

"But what if he asks us to stay?"

The plan was that if he asked, I'd keep my coat on the whole time *no matter what*. I tucked the green pants deeper into my boots and tried to disappear into my coat. When we went down to the Oval Office, from the corner of my eye I could see the official White House photographer lurking in the wings.

"Phyllis!" smiled President Carter, extending his hands. "Please come and sit down and chat with me a bit. And take off your coat."

"Oh, no, I'm *fine*, Mr. President. *Really*," I said, pulling the coat tighter around me. Then I sighed. Okay, this was ridiculous. Once again, it was time to come clean. I could only hope he'll think it's funny. "Well, Mr. President, the thing is I'm wearing your mother's pants!" I smiled and opened my coat wide for two seconds, giving him an eyeful of my golf-green polyester pants combined with my red sweater. Flash, flash, flash. The trusty White House photographer captured the moment on film forever.

Still, the president gazed at me, perplexed. "You're wearing my mother's pants?!"

"Oh, Mr. President," I sighed, "it's a lo-o-ong story."

And he looked at me and looked down at my outfit and—thank goodness—he started laughing. He had such a great sense of humor about it, and I explained the whole story as we sat in the Oval Office.

"Well," he said, "I guess my mother, as usual, came to the rescue!"

If the President of the United States can laugh at life's silly moments, I think we can too.

P.S.: Lincoln Tyler George Brown was born a few months after we slept in the Lincoln bedroom.

~

It's important to learn to not take things that other people say and do too seriously, either. Once when John and I were campaigning for the governorship in a small town in Kentucky, I ran into a corner drugstore to buy a new pair of panty hose since mine had a run. I ducked into the ladies' room to change and tossed the old pair in the trash can.

One enterprising drugstore clerk resurrected my torn panty hose from the trash, cut them up into little squares, and sold the pieces for a dollar a square. At first I was mortified. But before I got upset and let it ruin the day, I tried to look at the humor of the situation. My panty hose … strangers wanted to buy my ripped panty hose? How was he planning to sell them? When I imagined those squares of nylon being hawked on the streets of this small town, I started to see how bizarre the whole thing was and started to laugh about it. And the more I thought about it, the more I laughed. You have to appreciate this guy's entrepreneurial spirit. I hope he pulled in a bundle.

Then there was the time I rushed into a hotel rest room during the campaign to adjust my twisted panty hose (yes, I have hosiery issues!). The line for the stalls was twenty feet long and I only had a minute, so I broke in line, telling the women waiting that it was an emergency and there was no way I could "hold it in." They graciously said okay, and I slipped into a stall, adjusted my hose, flushed the toilet with my foot to keep up my pretense that it had been an emergency, and went back to the ballroom to greet more voters.

That is, until one woman approached me angrily. "I can't believe you did that!" she exclaimed loudly.

"Did what?" I was bewildered. I recognized her as one of the women waiting in the line.

"I can't believe you went to the bathroom and didn't wash your hands afterward. Now you're shaking everyone's hand! That's disgusting. What is my daughter going to think? Some example you are!"

"But … but … I didn't really *go* to the bathroom," I tried to explain.

She wouldn't hear it. "I heard you flush!"

"But I was only adjusting my panty hose."

My lord. My mother once said to me, "Be careful what you do in public, Phyllis, because there is always someone watching." She was right. ***There will always be people who are quick to criticize you no matter who you are or what you do. These comments usually come from other people's insecurities. Respond with humor and they'll lighten up, too.*** Whether it's your coworkers, your neighbors, or strangers—try to respond with a laugh.

My friend Rev. Mary Grace Williams is an expert at defusing criticism and performing punchy one-liners in one of the most serious of places—church. She is a former New York actress turned Episcopal priest who's had tough critics and has had to deal with many awkward moments. She does it by not taking herself too seriously.

"One of the questions I get all the time is: 'What do we call you? We can't call you 'Father.''" Mimi, as I call her, laughs. "And I always say that I prefer 'your Royal Highness.' People look at me as if to say, '*Is she serious?*' And then they laugh."

She can respond to any question with a light touch. "People also used to ask me, 'Why do you want to be a priest?' and I'd answer, 'Because I look stunning in black! With a touch of white at the throat! I had a choice: I could be a cocktail waitress or a priest, and let's be honest … they both work weekends

160 / NEVER SAY NEVER

and holidays, but the pension plan is better in the Episcopal church! And that black, it never goes out of fashion.'"

Mimi uses humor in her sermons too, though "people are not used to it. You have to be able to laugh about it all. If you have goof-ups at the altar, you just have to laugh it off … and these are moments that are sacred! To me, it's all about joy and celebrating life."

One Sunday a new family at her church had brought its rambunctious four-year-old to the service. All the children were sitting up front as Mimi gave them a special lesson on baptism and saints. "This little boy kept making comments," she says. "He was borderline disruptive."

But instead of telling him to stop, she paid the little boy a compliment. "I finally stopped, turned to him, and said, 'You know, Mark, I think you're going to be a priest.'" Dead silence. Then the child looked up at her and, in front of the whole parish, he said, "Oh, I can't be a priest." And Mimi asked him why not. And he said, "Because I'm a *guy*."

"My mouth fell open," says Mimi. "I looked down at him and then at the congregation and said, 'Well, I guess it's a new church!'"

Mimi believes firmly that humor has a place in the church and everywhere. "I think humor is a means by which to deal with all the horrible stuff we live with," she says. "It's a very healing thing. If we can't laugh, if we take ourselves too seriously, then we can't see beyond ourselves. And the whole point of our faith is to be beyond ourselves."

She is a great role model for all of us in using humor. We should follow her example when the barbs come our way.

The barbs certainly came my way when I became pregnant with my first child and everyone expected me to look like some sort of supermodel. But I'd never been the skinny-minny type anyway. John always used to call me a "big, strapping country girl," and I was generally in good shape—athletic, not scrawny. I had actually been shocked that I won the swimsuit category at the Miss America pageant. Because I thought I had no chance, I ate a steak and baked potato the night before that part of the competition.

When the pregnancy hormones kicked in, Queenie, one of the chefs at the governor's mansion, concocted a special recipe for chocolate Coca-Cola cake. Even today my mouth waters when I think about it. I have vivid memories of standing in the kitchen at 3 a.m. with spoon in hand, scooping cake straight from the pan and washing it down with a big glass of cold whole milk.

I did this for months. Hey, some people crave pickles; some are into peanut butter. Me? Chocolate cake, all the way. All the way up, up, up the scale until I had gained—are you ready for this?—seventy, that's "seven-o," pounds! And I loved every minute of it. It was the first time in my life I really enjoyed myself without worrying about every pound.

The press had a sweet time of it too. "TUBBY FLIES AND HUBBY SIGHS" was the headline in the newspaper one morning. I was still flying from Lexington, Kentucky, to New York every weekend to do *The NFL Today*; after all, I was still under contract. I found such publicity to be really mean-spirited, especially at such a wonderful time for me. And after a few headlines like that, people would stop me on the street and say right to my face, "Oh, Phyllis, you've gained so much weight!"

Okay, enough was enough! I was just as vulnerable as the next woman when it came to gaining weight and being self-conscious about my body. And I had to do it in public, on television, under the scrutiny of thousands of viewers. How was I supposed to get through this? How was I supposed to just brush off their words and not let it affect me? Where was the humor here? I decided to break down the criticisms. These people didn't know me. And their hurtful words were about something unimportant. Aside from my midnight cake raids, I was eating healthy good food (just a lot of it!), getting exercise, and doing just what the doctor ordered. I wasn't going to let the words of strangers spoil such a precious time for me. Surely they had better things to do? But if criticizing me made people feel better about themselves or gave them amusement, so be it. I decided people's focus on my weight was funny.

If they could have fun with it, so could I. I started to give out Queenie's famous and sinful chocolate Coca-Cola cake recipe to friends and whoever asked. Life can't be a series of rules (and diets) all the time. Have a little fun! Indulge yourself a bit! And here's where you can start ...

CHOCOLATE COCA-COLA CAKE

CAKE

2	cups flour
2	cups sugar
1	cup Coca-Cola
2	sticks margarine or butter
3	tablespoons cocoa
1 1/2	cups miniature marshmallows
1/2	cup buttermilk
2	eggs, well beaten
1	teaspoon baking soda
1	teaspoon vanilla extract

ICING

3   tablespoons cocoa
1   stick margarine or butter
6   tablespoons Coca-Cola
1   box powdered sugar
1   teaspoon vanilla extract

FOR CAKE

Combine flour and sugar and set aside. In a saucepan, combine and heat butter, cocoa, Coca-Cola, and marshmallows (add marshmallows last) until it begins to boil. Remove from heat and stir to dissolve marshmallows. Pour the mixture over sugar and flour mixture and blend well. Add buttermilk, eggs, baking soda, and vanilla, and blend well. Pour into greased 9 by 13 pan and bake at 350 degrees for 30 to 40 minutes. Ice while hot.

FOR ICING

Combine butter, cocoa, and Coca-Cola in saucepan and bring to a boil. Pour over powdered sugar, add vanilla, and blend well. Spread over cake. (Freezes nicely if necessary.)

My mouth is watering already. ***ENJOY!***

Afterword:
In Closing ...
a Few More Things

So now you know why saying "never say never" is so important to me. I'm in the middle of a rich, full, and interesting life—and there's still so much to come! In fact, since I am a here-and-now kind of person, it has sometimes felt strange to delve back into all of those memories and relive them again. We should never live in the past, but we must visit it every now and then in order to learn from it. Looking back, I realize that I am happy with the choices I've made. My son, Lincoln, has recently graduated from college and is starting out in business; my daughter, Pamela, has graduated from high school and is entering college. John and I divorced several years ago, but have remained friends. And here I am, a single woman living in New York, and, as always, ready for a whole new set of possibilities! Writing this book has given me the opportunity to reflect on the past while helping me prepare for the next phase.

I've also learned the importance of synergy through this book. The lessons I separated into ten chapters are truly not independent of each other. Instead, they intertwine and complement each other like that big crazy quilt I mentioned at the beginning. My wonderful friends whose stories you've read have also shown us how these lessons weave in and out of their lives and overlap whenever they have a decision to make or a challenge to face. You'll discover that too. If you say yes to yourself, you'll be prepared to embrace change. In order to find a void and fill it, you must be a risk taker and trust your instincts. Everything you do will be enhanced if you keep your options open and use the power of being nice. And when you face those times when life isn't perfect, you must learn to keep your perspective and be able to laugh at yourself.

In addition to those specific lessons, three themes run through their stories and mine. First, *dream big dreams*. Maybe, like Larry King, Barbara Taylor Bradford, and Johnny Bench, you had a dream as a child that you can make come true when you're an adult. Or maybe you have reached a certain point in your career, like Mayor Michael Bloomberg, Elaine Kaufman, Irv Cross, and Cathie Black, and can discover a new dream that gives the next stage of your life direction. Whenever or wherever you are, don't limit your dreams. Second, *turn your dreams into reality with your passion*. As you heard in the stories of Muhammad Ali, Roger Staubach, Jane Rosenthal, and Kathie Lee Gifford, you can't be lukewarm or half-hearted when you make up your mind to reach a major goal—you have to give it your all. And if you face obstacles like those that appeared in the paths of Liz Smith, Mary Hart, Walter Cronkite, Walter Anderson, Rick Pitino, and Paula Zahn, you must keep your enthusiasm and stay focused on the hard work and creativity needed to succeed. Third, *dare to be different*. Many successful people feel early in their lives that their dreams and their drive make them different from those around them. Later they come to realize that being different works for them, not against them, and they cultivate their special qualities to separate themselves from the crowd. As former Governor Ann Richards, Chris Evert, Senator Mary Landrieu, Richard Kirshenbaum, and Reverend Mary Grace Williams explained, they turned being different into being successful.

Every one of these people dreamed big, were passionate about achieving their goals, and dared to be different. Each of you reading this has the potential within you to do the same.

One of my favorite sayings is the oft-quoted "Yesterday is history, tomorrow is a mystery, and today is a gift—that's why we call it the present." One of the hardest things in life is to keep a healthy balance among all three: to learn from the past and plan for the future, while standing firmly in the present, appreciating each day as it comes.

So often we all try to do so much that we miss those small joys of the moment. I'm still working on doing that, but I've learned that part of the process is not trying to do everything. My daughter, Pamela, is especially good at helping me with this. She's constantly saying, "Mom, you try to be all things to all people and you are spreading yourself too thin! You shouldn't stress yourself out so much."

One weekend, all within forty-eight hours, Pamela's senior prom would be held at Henry Clay High School in Lexington, Kentucky; my son would graduate from the Wharton School of Business at the University of Pennsylvania; and my mother would have her eighty-third birthday on Mother's Day in Denton, Texas. I couldn't be in all three states at the same time.

Which one should I do? They all wanted me there, and I wanted to be there for them. So I sat on the floor for a while and boo-hooed in frustration. In the old days, I would have flown to Kentucky on Friday to see Pamela in her beautiful dress and take photos that evening; then fly to Denton on Saturday to take my mother out for dinner and surprise her with a birthday cake and gift; and then get on a plane again at a ridiculous hour Sunday morning to reach Philadelphia in time for Lincoln's graduation. On Monday, back in New York, I'd collapse.

Instead, this time, I took Pamela's advice and made some hard decisions. Since Lincoln's graduation was a once-in-a-lifetime event, I knew that had to be my priority, and I decided to share the entire weekend with him in Philadelphia. I sent my mother flowers and a gift and called to wish her happy birthday and promised to visit soon. And I told Pamela to get lots of pictures in her prom dress and call me on Saturday to tell me all about it. Freed from the stress of zipping around three places and knowing I would make it up to my mother and daughter later, I could relax and enjoy being with my son for this major turning point in his life.

Staying balanced is a constant effort, and enjoying the moment and setting priorities are only two of the many ways I try to do so. Some are things you may do as well: exercise, meditation, eating healthy, enjoying my "down time," keeping the faith, and constantly cultivating a good attitude. But the main thing that keeps me going is my hunger to learn. I'm like a sponge—open to everything around me, soaking it all in.

Having a healthy curiosity and an eagerness to learn helps you stay youthful and vigorous, no matter your age or your stage in life. Of course, being eager to learn something new requires a certain modesty—since you must also admit that there are things you don't know!

There is so much more I want to experience in life, so many new ways to grow, that I'm relentless in my determination not to miss anything. I don't know what will happen next. But that's part of the joy: I *never* know. I don't know what's around the corner ... and I can't wait. The possibilities are limitless.

I hope you will use the lessons in this book to help you think about the possibilities in your life and to help you balance your past, present, and future as well. If you do, you'll discover the deep satisfaction that comes from knowing you're growing every day. As Oliver Wendell Holmes said, "The great thing in life is not where we are, but where we are going." This is just as true today as it was in the nineteenth century.

Who knows what *you* will do tomorrow or where you will be next year? Your possibilities may be different from mine, but if you keep yourself open to new ideas, anything is possible. Find something you want to do, and when someone tells you that you'll never do it, prove them wrong. And if you're tempted to say to yourself you'll never do something, stop, think about all the stories you've read in this book and say, "I can do this." Throw all the "can'ts," "no's," and "nevers" out of your life. You can do it! Just keep saying, "Yes, I can!"

ACKNOWLEDGMENTS

Many people who have been part of my life have contributed to the making of this book. First and foremost, I thank my parents, Bob and Louise, and my children, Lincoln and Pamela, for their love, support, inspiration, and patience. My beloved father ("Bob-Bob," as his five grandchildren called him) passed away six years ago, but his spirit will always be with me. This book is dedicated to them.

At my fiftieth birthday party a few years ago, one of my favorite people, Barbara Walters, suggested I find a way to share my advice with others drawing from my diverse life experiences. Shortly thereafter, my friend Maria Shriver, who was completing her own inspirational book at the time, also encouraged me to share some of my life lessons. She suggested I write a book. Later, Maria gave me valuable advice on all aspects of putting a book together. Then, over lunch one day, my long-time friend, Walter Anderson, discussed with me several ideas for new projects I was considering. He asked me what I felt most passionate about. After thinking about it, I said my "never say never" message. *Bingo!* Suddenly, my decision about my next project was becoming very clear. Joe Armstrong, my Texas soul brother, was also at that lunch. Joe and I have been pals forever and have been there for each other through thick and thin. He also thought it would be a great idea to do a book and has provided an amazing support system for me throughout this entire process. More than anything, he makes me laugh. Thank you, Barbara, Maria, Walter, and Joe, for your encouragement.

A very special note of gratitude goes to Rick Pitino—a very successful motivational author and speaker himself—for the wonderful foreword. I met Rick and his family when I was living in Lexington, Kentucky. Rick was the head basketball coach at the University of Kentucky and led the Wildcats to an exciting national championship. Rick, your kind words are much too generous! Thank you so much.

I also want to thank Charles Gargano, who was a pillar of strength for me when I moved back to New York City. He will always be a very special person in my life.

Several other friends read some or all of the book in manuscript form and helped me clarify points and reconstruct scenes from the past. Thank you to my dear friends Sheila Jefferson, Dr. Jane Greer, Louis Schmidt, Mike Pearl, Kate Edelman Johnson, Kerry Kramp, Denise O'Connor, Carol Butler, and John Y. Brown.

My hairstylist Vincent Roppatte, whom I've worked with since I was Miss America, has been a loyal friend and part of my "family" for many years now. I treasure his friendship and thank him for using his magic touch to always help me look my best—

and therefore feel incredible. Vincent has been a part of every major project I've ever done, including the cover of this book.

John Zannikos and my friends at Three Guys Restaurant, my favorite New York diner, provided constant encouragement, my favorite booth (where I wrote my introduction!), and nourishment that helped more than they know. An occasional slice of pound cake topped with fat-free vanilla frozen yogurt and fat-free chocolate sauce when I was nervous about the book was particularly helpful and gave me a much-needed burst of energy.

Natasha Stoynoff played a key role in the development of this book. With her warm personality and superb interviewing skills, Natasha helped me dig deep to remember episodes and details. Her expertise in tracking down biographical data, helping me craft stories, and developing punch lines was also invaluable. You started out as a collaborator, Natasha, but you became a friend. Even though you are from Canada, I am making you an honorary "southern belle" because of your fascination with anything southern. Thank you.

Thanks to my literary agent, Lynn Whittaker, whom I met when we worked on my story for the book *Making Waves: The 50 Greatest Women in Radio & Television*. We hit it off so well that I knew instantly I wanted to work with her on this project. From my late night to early morning phone calls, Lynn has "held my hand" through this entire process. She believed in me when there were times I questioned myself. Her kindness, sound judgment, "southernness," and wonderful laugh have gotten me through this project. She was a great sounding board for me. She patiently allowed me to "go through my process" (then reconsider when I had second thoughts), indulged me when I needed to vent, and guided me in deciding what to include and how far to go. She constantly reminded me whenever I was getting stressed out over whether I could pull this off that I had to sit back and "laugh at myself"—Lesson #10! She's a saint.

One of the best things Lynn did for me and this book was to lead us into the capable hands of Nancy Hancock, my editor at McGraw-Hill. Nancy's immediate, intuitive understanding of my message made her an instant kindred spirit. Her wise editorial judgment and her keen marketing sense have been absolutely instrumental in helping this book be all it can be. I'm also grateful for her calm confidence and her patience, which I have sorely tested at times! My sincerest gratitude goes as well to the entire team at McGraw-Hill who have been supportive, creative, and smart in their handling of this book and very nice to me. Special kudos to Philip Ruppel, Lynda Luppino, Lydia Rinaldi, David Dellaccio, Meg Leder, Scott Kurtz, and the entire sales team.

Thanks to my long-time loyal assistant and dear friend, Dee Emmerson, who has been involved in so many chapters of my life for over twenty years. From my years at CBS in New York, to Kentucky, to the present, Dee has been the efficient and capable "staff of one" who has held everything and everyone together. She deftly runs "command central" with her amazing people skills and juggles more job descriptions than anyone could ever believe. Dee is also one of the loveliest people I've ever known. How she puts up with me I'll never know! Dee, you have an everlasting place in my family's heart, especially mine.

A special thank you as well to all my close friends who have had incredible patience with me during my work on this book. Thanks, everyone! I can't wait to pick up where we left off.

I was able to write this book because of the positive attitude that I was lucky enough to develop at earlier stages in my life and have never lost. So I also want to thank all the people who have inspired and taught me along the way. This starts with all the folks in Denton, Texas, my hometown, who believed in me early on and have been behind me all the way. Special individual thanks go to my speech teacher at Denton High School, Opal Hall, who first helped me identify my special abilities and gave me the confidence to pursue my dreams; to Dr. Isabel Scionti, my piano teacher, who believed in my talent and taught me discipline and that "practice, practice, practice makes perfect!"; and to Ema Ruth Russell, my choir teacher, who helped me realize I was an alto, all right, but that I should stick to the piano!

And a special thank you to the late Dr. Norman Vincent Peale, who was a wonderful teacher and friend to me and whose spirit lives on in everything I do. Both of my children were christened by Dr. Peale at the historic Marble Collegiate Church in New York City. To Dr. Peale and your wonderful wife, Ruth, who is carrying on your message: I'm still trying to follow your lead! I hope you're pleased.

Finally, my sincere gratitude goes to my extraordinary friends who generously responded to my request for their favorite "never say never" story from their lives: Muhammad Ali, Walter Anderson, Johnny Bench, Cathie Black, Mayor Michael Bloomberg, Barbara Taylor Bradford, Walter Cronkite, Irv Cross, Chris Evert, Kathie Lee Gifford, Mary Hart, Elaine Kaufman, Larry King, Richard Kirshenbaum, Senator Mary Landrieu, Rick Pitino, Governor Ann Richards, Jane Rosenthal, Liz Smith, Roger Staubach, the Reverend Mary Grace Williams, and Paula Zahn. They are very busy and successful people who took time out of their schedules either to do interviews with me or write their own stories for the book. What they contributed to this book involves much more than time. By sharing their personal stories with us, they candidly and graciously opened a window into their successes and failures. These people inspire us all, not only with their stories but also with their willingness to share a part of themselves. Thank you, my friends.

ABOUT THE AUTHOR

Phyllis George first came into the national spotlight when she was crowned Miss America 1971. Since then, she has had an eclectic career spanning several different fields.

In television, she was the first woman to have an ongoing role as a national sportscaster, co-hosting the Emmy-winning *NFL Today* on CBS from 1974 to 1984 and interviewing many of the greatest sports figures in the world. She also co-hosted three Super Bowl broadcasts and six Rose Bowl Parades. Since then, she has been co-anchor of the *CBS Morning News* and host of two series on TNN, *Spotlight with Phyllis George* and *Woman's Day TV with Phyllis George.* In 2000, she had her first acting role in the box office hit *Meet the Parents.*

From 1979 to 1983, while serving as First Lady of Kentucky, she became a devoted supporter of hand-made crafts. She established the Kentucky Art & Craft Foundation, which became a role model for other organizations around the country, and subsequently hosted a series on QVC, *American Crafts with Phyllis George,* for eight years.

In 1986, she became the first woman to found her own chicken company, Chicken by George, a line of healthy, boneless, skinless, marinated breasts that launched a whole new trend in the food industry. Chicken by George is now a division of Hormel Foods.

American Women in Radio and Television named her one of the "50 Greatest Women in Radio & Television" in 2001. Her biography and her personal essay about being a sportscaster appear in *Making Waves: The 50 Greatest Women in Radio & TV* (Andrews McMeel, 2001). She is also the author of three illustrated books on quilts and other American crafts.

Among other honors, Phyllis was named one of the "Leading Women Entrepreneurs of the World" in 2001; the first female recipient of the Jack Quinlan Award for Excellence in Sport Broadcasting in 1985; and NAWBO's National Celebrity Businesswoman of the Year in 1991. Save the Children gave her a "Distinguished Service Award" in 1994 for more than 20 years of service, and in 2003, she received the Norman Vincent Peale Award for Positive Thinking. In 2006, the Alzheimer's Association presented Phyllis with the prestigious Rita Hayworth Award for her passionate advocacy on behalf of people, like her own mother, who suffer from Alzheimer's disease.